Sports Illustrated

WOMEN'S GYMNASTICS 1:

The Floor Exercise Event

THE SPORTS ILLUSTRATED LIBRARY

BOOKS ON TEAM SPORTS

Baseball	Football: Defense	Pitching
Basketball	Football: Offense	Soccer
Curling: Techniques and Strategy	Football: Quarterback	Volleyball
	Ice Hockey	

BOOKS ON INDIVIDUAL SPORTS

Badminton	Skiing	*Women's Gymnastics 2: The Vaulting,
*Bowling	Squash	Balance Beam, and
Fly Fishing	Table Tennis	Uneven Parallel
Golf	*Tennis	Bars Events
Handball	Track: Field Events	Wrestling
Horseback Riding	Track: Running Events	
Judo	*Women's Gymnastics 1: The Floor	
*Racquetball		
*Running for Women	Exercise Event	

BOOKS ON WATER SPORTS

Powerboating	Small Boat Sailing
*Scuba Diving	Swimming and Diving
Skin Diving and Snorkeling	

SPECIAL BOOKS

*Backpacking	Safe Driving
Dog Training	Training with Weights

*EXPANDED FORMAT

Sports Illustrated

WOMEN'S GYMNASTICS 1:
The Floor Exercise Event

by Don Tonry with Barbara Tonry

Illustrations by Don Tonry

LIPPINCOTT & CROWELL, PUBLISHERS

New York

SPORTS ILLUSTRATED WOMEN'S GYMNASTICS 1: THE FLOOR EXERCISE EVENT. Copyright © 1980 by Time Inc.
FIRST EDITION

Library of Congress Cataloging in Publication Data

Tonry, Don.
  Sports illustrated women's gymnastics.
  (The Sports illustrated library)
  CONTENTS: v. 1. The floor exercise event.—
v. 2. The vaulting, balance beam, and uneven parallel bars events.
  1. Gymnastics for women—Collected works.
I. Tonry, Barbara, joint author. II. Title.
III. Title: Women's gymnastics.
GV464.T62   796.4'1   79-25050
ISBN 0-690-01908-4 (v. 1)
ISBN 0-690-01907-6 (v. 1) pbk.
ISBN 0-690-01909-2 (v. 2)
ISBN 0-690-01906-8 (v. 2) pbk.

---

80 81 82 83 84 10 9 8 7 6 5 4 3 2 1

Contents

3. Floor Exercise Skills: Tumbling and Acrobatics 55

4. Dance and the Floor Exercise Event 133

5. Selected Floor Exercise Combinations 169

Introduction

Sports Illustrated Women's Gymnastics has been written in two parts. Both books are intended for the young female gymnast and should be used together as an introduction to the women's Olympic Gymnastics All-Around Program. This book instructs the performer in general conditioning for gymnastics, and teaches the floor exercise event by carefully outlining the necessary steps for training through progressive levels of expertise. This "starter text" also guides the beginner in such matters as safety, spotting methods, strength and flexibility exercises, and basic positions and movements. The second book covers the other three events of the Olympic gymnastics program for women: the vaulting, balance beam, and uneven parallel bars events.

The overhead projection method was used to illustrate both books. Films of top Olympic, World Championship, and National level gymnasts in performance were gathered and studied for more than a year before selected frames were reproduced on the drawing board. Together, the two books contain more than 400 illustrations and well over 2,000 individual figures.

TO THE GYMNAST

This book has been written and illustrated for you, the female gymnast. It is an attempt to pass on some of the information accumulated from the author's long experience as a gymnast and gymnastics teacher. Keep in mind that a book on gymnastics, no matter how well written and illustrated, will never be able to answer all of your questions, and cannot replace a good coach or dance instructor. However, this book should give you the basic instruction you will need to get started, and will keep you thinking about and practicing new skills.

Memorize the section entitled "Safety in the Gym." If you do not follow these common sense rules, you will acquire bad habits that only invite trouble.

A section on spotting (physically assisting the gymnast) has been included for both you and your coach. Every gymnast must rely on help from someone else when attempting to execute a new skill. Make sure your spotter knows exactly what you are about to do and is capable of assisting you correctly. Do not let just anyone spot you. First judge the spotter's competence by watching him or her help other performers and by considering the spotter's coaching experience.

Proceed with the first chapter, which begins with a discussion of four basic strength exercises for the development of key muscle groups important to gymnastic performance. These exercises will both help you get in shape to perform the basic skills and increase your strength as your training progresses.

Learn all of the flexibility exercises in each category. They are designed to improve the suppleness of specific muscles that are heavily used in skill performance.

Follow the pattern outlined at the beginning of the next section, entitled "The Workout." This procedure will give you a controlled, well-organized training session. A coach can always spot a beginner in the gym by the way she jumps from one thing to another in no logical sequence and without warming up properly. (Beginners are also characterized by their overuse of paraphernalia such as tape, wrist wraps, kneeguards, headbands, and so on. Most experienced gymnasts find these accessories a cumbersome distraction.)

Learn the "Basic Positions and Movements" that are common in most skills. When you are able to assume the positions quickly and easily, try them with movements so that you can begin to feel how they relate to each other.

"Learning the Handstand" appears early in the book because the aspiring young gymnast should learn this skill as soon as possible. The handstand is perhaps the most important "core skill" in the sport of gymnastics. This section also introduces the concept of step-by-step progression in learning a skill.

A brief history of the floor exercise event begins the second chapter. It is useful to know how what you are doing began and how it became what it is today. This is followed by a discussion of floor exercise composition, and by an explanation of direction of movement in gymnastics.

The third chapter teaches the beginning gymnast to perform the floor exercise skills. The approximate level of difficulty is indicated for each. Based on the author's personal experience, the skills are rated from one (elementary) to ten (advanced) in order to alert the reader to the degree of proficiency required to perform each skill. A skill with a relatively high rating such as a 5 or 6 probably requires more balance, coordination, strength, and experience than a skill rated 2 or 3. It is best to proceed one step at a time and not attempt the more difficult skills without adequate preparation.

There are detailed descriptions of the skills. The reader may notice that some of the accompanying illustrations do not demonstrate the most elementary form of a particular skill. World class gymnasts often add their distinctive styles to basic skills, and these personal touches have been included in some illustrations to enhance the basic skill and demonstrate the possibilities for embellishment.

Prerequisite skills are indicated after most descriptions so that the reader can determine whether or not she is ready to attempt the new skill. If the student does not know how to perform the prerequisites, she should learn them before attempting to master the new skill.

Special instructions on spotting are included in the discussions of many skills.

Variations of core skills are presented frequently to give the reader an understanding of possible modifications and elaborations of basic skills. Usually, the variations are not described in great detail because they duplicate the core skill patterns, to some extent, and are illustrated.

The fourth chapter discusses dance elements included in the floor exercise event, and the fifth chapter presents selected floor exercise combinations.

Remember, learn all of the basic skills (those with a skill level of 1) before proceeding to the more difficult ones.

TO THE COACH

Beginning coaches will find this book a valuable aide in improving their general knowledge of the sport and its spotting techniques. In addition to safety and spotting procedures, features of particular interest to coaches are the selected conditioning exercises, basic procedure during the workout, skill descriptions and illustrations, and specification of the prerequisites of each skill.

Experienced coaches will appreciate the accurate illustrations, based on films of the world's best gymnasts. These illustrations will enable coaches to quickly show their students exactly how the skills are executed. It is hoped that coaches will also find many new and interesting bits of information on spotting, training, and performance.

The gymnastics coach has one of the most difficult and time-consuming jobs in the world of coaching. In order to teach effectively, he or she must spend hours not only explaining and exhorting, but also pushing, pulling, holding, and catching performers. In addition, while coaches of other sports rely primarily on strategy and talent during the competition, the gymnastics coach must also depend on choreography, since choreography plays a major roll in determining an individual's (or team's) score. Moreover, because the entire performance is prearranged to suit the ability of the performer, gymnastics is not a game or race that can be coached by the whistle or stop watch. It is a sport in which the coach must teach an enormous number of complicated movements and patterns that incorporate *all* possible planes and axes of the body. The gymnastics coach must understand the composition of routines, the biomechanics of movement, the relationships among various skills, how to teach a skill step by step, spotting techniques, music, dance, technical execution and the general and specific rules of competition. Gymnastics coaches have to constantly improve old skills and spend hours manually and verbally teaching new ones. The end result is judged on the basis of not only technical execution but also imaginative and innovative composition.

SAFETY IN THE GYM

Safety in the gym is more important to the beginning gymnast than any other consideration. Paying attention to the rules of safety minimizes the likelihood of injury and creates the best atmosphere in which to learn the necessary skills as quickly and easily as possible. Please heed them:

- Warm up adequately at the beginning of each workout and before attempting specific skills.
- Be certain the apparatus and mats are adjusted and secured correctly. Make sure there is an adequate number of mats and that they lie flat with no large cracks between them.

- Get assistance from a spotter when it is logical to do so. Do not guess about your ability to execute a new skill; ask someone who knows.
- Be sure you have mastered all of the preliminary steps before trying a new skill.
- Never work out alone. Always be sure a gymnastics coach is in the gym. A basketball coach will not do.
- Take advantage of every safety device available in the gym, even if you need to use them only a couple of times before you are ready to perform without any help.
- Be sure fast first aid and more substantial medical care are available at a moment's notice. If you are injured even slightly, attend to it promptly.
- Do not use tape on ankles, wrists, forearms, and hands as preventive measures unless such aides have been prescribed by a coach, trainer, nurse, or doctor. You will become dependent on these bandages for support and feel lost when they are not available. Try to avoid relying on gimmicks and developing idiosyncrasies while training.
- If you begin to feel excessive stress or pain in your wrists, lower back, or elsewhere, stop. You must increase your strength and flexibility carefully over a long period of time until you have properly conditioned your body.

SPOTTING

Spotting means manually supporting and otherwise assisting a performer through a skill or series of skills. The purposes of spotting are to accelerate the learning process by providing physical help to the gymnast, and to insure safety.

Following are several important considerations in spotting.

- The gymnast *and* the coach should first judge their ability to perform their respective tasks; if either party is deficient a disaster may occur.
- The performer should understand the basic technique of a skill before attempting it.
- The performer must be able to do the prerequisite skills.
- Break the skill down into small steps, utilizing any additional aides necessary, such as the floor, trampoline, and rolled-up mats.
- Spot the performer very carefully (get help if there are physical or psychological reasons for a double spot) until it is apparent that the performer's confidence and physical ability are sufficient.

Spotting Methods

Two basic techniques are used in spotting: hand spotting and belt spotting. Hand spotting, in which the coach uses his hands to support or push various parts of the student's body as she attempts a new skill, is the more common because it is convenient and provides help to the performer in a greater variety of subtle situations. On the other hand, the belt spot—support by means of a belt and suspended ropes—is much more effective for skills that are performed on a high bar or require a great amount of physical and/or psychological aid. The decision to use one method or the other depends on which provides the most assistance and safety in the performance of the skill, and on an evaluation of the possible psychological help each method may give the performer. Employing both methods properly requires considerable training.

Hand Spotting

Hand spotting is used extensively at the very beginning of a gymnast's training, when the novice is placed in the various positions that will be assumed during the performance of the skills. This approach allows the coach to learn right along with the gymnast. Eventually the coach will begin to "feel" all of the gymnast's weaknesses in a particular movement. The instructor must also learn how much force to use in assisting the performer through a specific skill. Although it is usually safer to overspot than to provide insufficient help, too much assistance can be dangerous and may also retard the student's development of self-reliance. Thus, spotting should be provided only where and when it is necessary.

Generally, the hip area—the performer's center of gravity—is the focal point in spotting most skills. This body region is supported or pushed as the gymnast practices a new skill. Pushing or supporting the hips does not disturb the general body position as much as pushing a higher or lower part of the body. Naturally, there are many occasions when it is desirable to support or thrust more than one body part in order to keep the performer on course and her limbs in correct position. A good spotter has the ability to provide aid several times and in several different places during the performance of a single skill.

Belt Spotting

There are two basic kinds of spotting belts: twisting belts and non-twisting belts. Twisting belts are almost always used for *advanced* twisting skills.

In this type of spotting, a belt is buckled around the waist of the gymnast. Attached to each side of the belt is a rope that rises to the ceiling. Both ropes

Belt Spotting

curve around a pully system attached to the ceiling and then drop together to the floor, where the spotter grips the ropes with both hands and pulls down on them at the moment the gymnast's feet leave the floor as she begins the skill. This supports the performer while she is in the air, aids her rotation, and prevents a bad fall if she fails to execute the skill properly.

Although this overhead pulley rigging is preferable, many gyms do not have this type of belt spotting facility. If the overhead rigging is not possible, the safety belt spot must be administered by two individuals standing on each side of the performer and holding the belt ropes.

Follow these rules when belt spotting with an overhead rigging:

- The gymnast must be free and clear of the two ropes throughout her performance of the skill. Tangled ropes may hurt the gymnast. To prevent this, carefully review the movements of the skill with reference to the positions of the ropes. A sweat suit may be worn to prevent a possible rope burn.
- For a smooth, steady pull during the performance, adjust the ropes before the skill is attempted. Do not allow the ropes to be slack as the skill is begun, and always start by holding the ropes with your hands above your shoulder level so that you will have more leverage and a greater range of motion for pulling downward.
- Attempt to pull the ropes with a timing and force appropriate to the movement of the gymnast. Pulling too hard or at the wrong moment may spoil what would have been a good performance.
- Land the gymnast! The spotter's grip on the rope should not be completely relaxed as the landing occurs.

Additional Spotting Aids

Mats or commercial Styrofoam platforms can be used by the spotter to gain additional elevation while spotting "hard to reach" skills. Be sure any elevated spotting surface is stable.

Mounds of very soft landing mats can often replace a spotter. In this case, the gymnast receives assistance mainly in the landing phase of a particular skill.

1

Preparing for Gymnastic Training

Almost anyone can learn to perform gymnastic skills. The basic prerequisites are *strength* and *flexibility*. Performing the following exercises regularly will give the beginning performer the necessary minimum of both.

STRENGTH

(1) Do three push-ups on the floor with the body held absolutely straight. Push-ups may be performed from the hands-and-knees position until enough strength is acquired to permit push-ups from hands and toes. Do not allow your hips to sag as you move up or down.

(2) Do ten leg raises, lifting your legs from the floor to a vertical position while lying on your back. Your legs should be held absolutely straight throughout, and your lower back should be kept flat on the floor.

(3) Try leg raises while hanging from a horizontal bar if your stomach muscles are strong enough. Hold your legs straight and jerk them upward toward the bar until you gain enough strength to raise them slowly and smoothly.

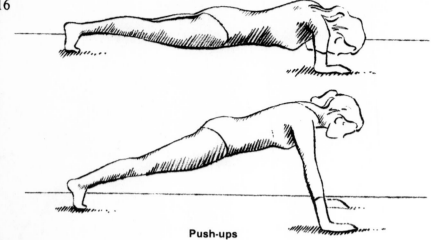

Push-ups

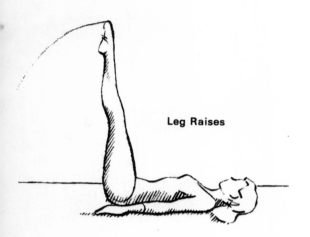

Leg Raises

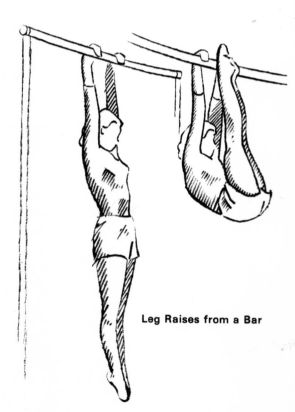

Leg Raises from a Bar

Pull-ups

(4) Do one pull-up (palms backward or forward) while hanging from a horizontal bar with thumbs held opposite forefingers. Have a partner assist you during the pull-up phase if you have trouble getting started. Always lower your body with a slow, even motion.

It is best to do these strength exercises *after* rather than before you begin each practice session so that you will not be worn out before you begin the workout. They should not be omitted even if you can do them easily. A fairly strong gymnast should be able to at least triple the number of repetitions prescribed here as a minimum.

The push-ups will help you to keep your arms straight in the handstand and support positions. The leg raises will strengthen your stomach and other hip-bending muscles so that you can lift your legs quickly on kips and rolls.

The pull-ups will add strength to your shoulders and arm flexors (pulling muscles), enabling you to pull yourself upward easily when this action is necessary.

FLEXIBILITY

Flexibility exercises are often done too aggressively by the beginning gymnast. There are no shortcuts that will give you flexibility fast. It is a *slow* process of *carefully* stretching various muscles just enough to bring gradual improvement. When in a stretch position, either hold the position for several seconds or bounce softly. Remember, a muscle that has been overstretched will react by tightening up.

Unlike the exercises for strength, the following flexibility exercises should be done *before* each practice session, with some stretching afterward as well.

Leg Muscles

To stretch the inside and rear thigh muscles, *splitting* exercises are required. It is helpful (but not essential) to be able to do a split with either the right or left leg forward; if you cannot perform it both ways, you may want to make it one of your goals.

(1) Lie on your back with your lower back held flat on the floor. Gently bring one leg up and hold your foot with your hands for ten seconds in a slightly uncomfortable split position. Perform this exercise three times with each leg.
(2) While holding on to a support, gently raise one leg to the rear as high as possible and push backward. This action will help to strengthen your lower back as well as increase your flexibility in the split position.
(3) Place one foot forward on a support with your rear foot flat on the floor behind your hips. Gently bend forward and hold this position for ten seconds. Do this three times.

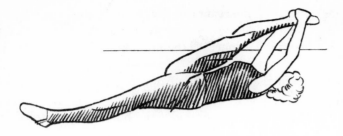

Split from Supine Position

Standing Split, Leg Raised to Rear

Forward Stretch with Front Leg Supported

Now you are ready for several split-sitting exercises.

(4) Split and stretch backward to further increase the flexibility of the rear leg and hip joint.

(5) Split and bend the rear leg to further stretch the front thigh muscles in the rear leg.

(6) Split and bend forward for additional stretching of the hamstring muscles in the forward leg.

(7) Assume a straddle position and gently lower your stomach to the floor while using your arms for support. This skill is harder to perform than a split. Move slowly and be patient.

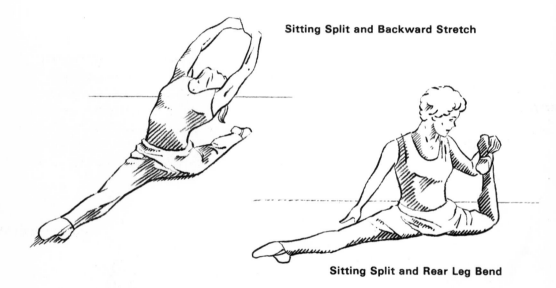

Sitting Split and Backward Stretch

Sitting Split and Rear Leg Bend

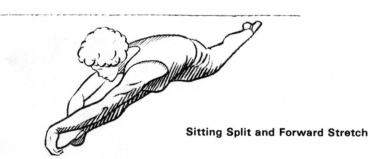

Sitting Split and Forward Stretch

Back Muscles

(1) Start by lying on the floor on your back. Place your hands below your shoulders, bend your knees, and push up to a *bridge*. A flexible performer can straighten her arms and bring her shoulders directly over her hands. Build up your bridging flexibility slowly over a period of weeks. Always push up slowly so that you can feel your tolerance for stretching in this position.

(2) If you are comfortable in the bridge position, practice raising one leg to a

Bridge

Bridge, Practice Kick

vertical position. Eventually you can learn to kick over through a split handstand position to a landing on one foot.

(3) To stand from a bridge position, increase the bend in your knees and rock forward toward your feet. Lead with your hips and keep your back arched until you are standing straight up.

(4) To go from a stand back down to a bridge, lean backward and slowly lower your upper body as you gently thrust your hips forward. Maintain your balance as your hands approach the floor.

Bridge to Standing Position

Leg and Back Muscles

The following exercises stretch the muscles in the backs of your legs and lower back area.

(1) Sit with straight legs and bend forward, leading with your stomach. Round your upper back as late as possible and hold your toes for ten seconds. Execute this exercise three times.

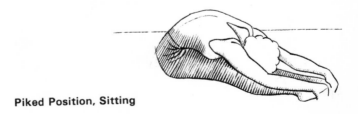

Piked Position, Sitting

(2) Lie on your back and raise your legs over your head without bending your knees. Gently press your toes to the floor. Hold this position for ten seconds. Do this three times.

(3) Gently bend forward from a standing position without bending your knees. You may grasp your ankles or hold your arms outstretched as illustrated. Maintain this position for ten seconds. Do this exercise three times.

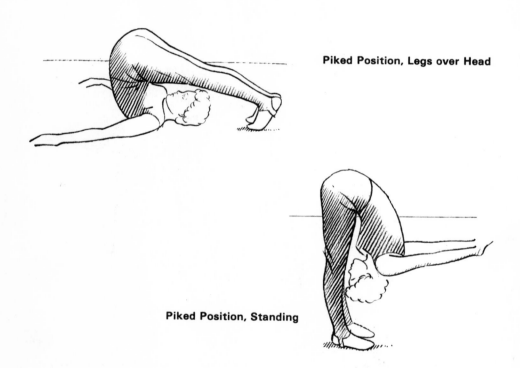

Piked Position, Legs over Head

Piked Position, Standing

Waist and Shoulders

These exercises involve side stretching while standing and shoulder stretching while hanging.

(1) For the side stretch, stand with your legs apart and stretch upward and sideways with a gentle bouncing motion. Do this exercise ten times on each side.

(2) To stretch your shoulders, hang from a horizontal bar or from the high bar of the uneven parallel bars apparatus as in the illustration. Use an *eagle grip:* the arms are twisted and positioned somewhat behind you, and palms face rearward. Relax your shoulders and hang in this position for ten seconds.

(3) Grasp a bar about shoulder height in an eagle grip. Hang with your arms straight, knees bent, and feet on the floor. Using your feet to push and pull, gently move your shoulders backward behind your hands and then forward in front of your hands. Perform this exercise ten times.

Side Stretch

Eagle Grip Hang

Eagle Grip Stretch

THE WORKOUT

The gymnast must follow a basic routine or procedure during every workout. In addition, she should plan the specifics of each training session in advance. Spend some time studying the instructions on how to perform the skills you intend to practice that day. If you have a coach, discuss your workout with her or him daily.

Follow this basic procedure in every workout:

(1) Begin your warm-up by jogging or jumping (three to five minutes) until you are breathing heavily and almost sweating. Before jogging, stretch your calf muscles. Take a big step backward and gently press your heel to the floor, with a bouncing motion, about fifteen times. Repeat this with the other leg and foot.

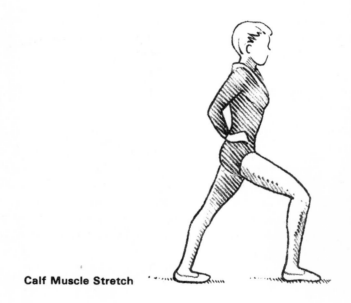

Calf Muscle Stretch

(2) Do the stretching exercises (five to ten minutes).
(3) Before starting to work on the first skill to be practiced, warm up further with simple but important fundamentals. Any additional stretching that is specific to the event should take place during this time (five to ten minutes).
(4) Work on new skills, old skills, or a particular routine according to how far

along you are in training (thirty to sixty minutes). Work on one event at a time unless the gym is crowded and you must move on to another event in order to give others enough room to practice.

(5) After the event workout, finish the session with five minutes of stretching, five minutes of strength exercises, and running.

BASIC POSITIONS AND MOVEMENTS

It is difficult to be a beginner in any sport, but most experts agree that floor exercise activity gives the neophyte the best and easiest possible introduction to gymnastics. Floor exercise is the broad term used to describe almost any gymnastic movement that can be performed on mats without the use of any additional apparatus.

There are four basic positions—the tucked, piked, layout, and arched positions—that every beginner should be able to assume while standing or sitting on the floor. The ability to perform these positions is essential to learning every skill in the gymnastics program.

Tucked Position

This position is used to speed up the rotation of your body while performing a forward or backward somersault.

To assume this position, sit on the floor and grasp the lower legs just below the knees. Your legs should be held together and your back should be rounded. Practice rolling backward so that your head touches the mat, and then forward to the sitting tucked position again. Try to roll forward with enough force to enable you to stand on your feet immediately after returning to the sitting tucked position.

Tucked Position, Sitting

Try to execute several tucked jumps from a standing position. Swing your arms forward and upward as you jump. Emphasize the tightness of the tuck and the fast release of the legs before landing.

Tucked Jump

Piked Position

It is more difficult to somersault in a piked position than in a tucked position because your limbs are extended away from your center of gravity, or point of rotation (the approximate middle of your body), and thus your rotation is slower.

To assume the piked position, sit on the floor and raise your legs while your arms support you from behind. Keep your legs straight and the pike as tight as possible.

Sitting Piked Position with Supporting Arms

To jump in a piked position, start with your arms held overhead. When you jump, swing your arms downward and then out behind you while bending at the hips and extending the legs as shown.

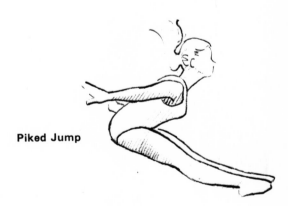

Piked Jump

Layout Position

This position eliminates the lower back arch and should be used in all skills that require straight body alignment, such as the handstand.

Recline on your back and extend your arms above your head. Tighten your seat muscles and press your lower back almost flat on the floor. Make yourself as long as possible.

Practice jumping in the layout position, keeping your body as straight as possible. Try to tighten your seat muscles and flatten your lower back as before. Watch the mat in front of you during the jump, and bend your knees as you land.

Layout Position

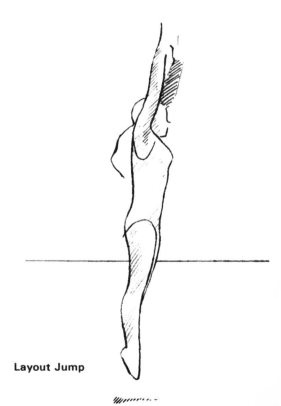

Layout Jump

Arched Position

To assume the arched position, lie on your stomach with your arms held forward or out to the side, arch your back, and tense your seat muscles. As you arch, make yourself as long as possible.

To jump in the arched position, arch your back and watch the mat as you jump so that you know where you are at all times. Bend your knees on landing.

Arched Position

Arched Jump

Straddle

The straddle is often used in conjunction with the pike, layout, and arch in various skills. Practice jumping in the basic positions described above—with the exception of the tuck—while your legs are straddled as wide as possible. Do not forget to bring your legs together for the landing.

Straddle Jump

After several days of practicing these basic positions, try to incorporate some of them into the following movements:

From a front support position with arched back, jump to a squat position and then straighten to a stand.

Squat to Stand

From a front support position with arched back, jump with your legs straight to a stand.

Pike to Stand

From a front support position with arched back, squat between your arms and then move to a sit with rear support.

Squat to Sit

From a sit, execute a half turn through a side support to a front support position, then another half turn through a side support to a rear support or sitting position.

From a layout position on your back, raise your legs and upper body and touch your toes in a V (piked) position.

From a piked position on your back with most of your weight resting on your shoulders, *kip* upward to a bridge position by quickly extending your hips, pushing with your arms, and arching your back.

Sit to Full Turn to Sit

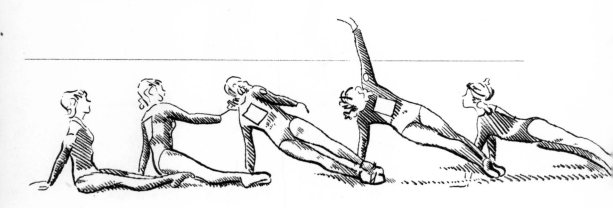

Layout Position to Sitting Piked Position

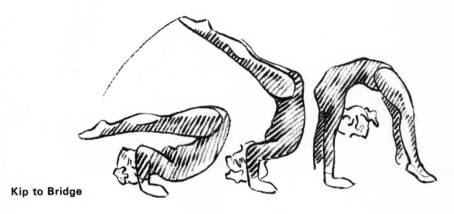

Kip to Bridge

LEARNING THE HANDSTAND

Every skill can be broken down into its component parts, or into simpler, subsidiary skills to be learned as a way of leading up to mastery of the more difficult skill. This procedure teaches the gymnast each skill in a safe and logical manner. The more difficult the skill, the more numerous and detailed the progressive steps should be.

Even Olympic gymnasts divide skills into small steps or units so that they can learn each unit to perfection. A top gymnast knows that a judge will watch her performance closely to see that each detail is done properly.

In most of the discussions of the various skills in Chapter 3, note the recommended minimum requirements for a particular skill, which are given under the heading "Prerequisites." These more elementary skills are the steps by which the beginner advances until she is able to begin practicing the skill.

The following procedure in learning the all-important handstand will serve as an example of how to learn a skill step by step.

Knee-Elbow Headstand

(1) Squat with your knees apart and place your hands on the mat between your knees, about shoulder width apart.

(2) Bend your elbows further and rest the inner part of your knees on your elbows or upper arms. Then watch the mat as you slowly and carefully lean forward and gently place the front part of the top of your head on the mat about eight inches in front of your hands. Hold this position for five seconds and return to the starting position.

Knee-Elbow Headstand

Knee-Elbow Handstand

This maneuver is the same as the knee-elbow headstand except that this time the head is not lowered to the mat. Slowly lean forward with your head held up so that you can watch the area of the mat in front of your hands. Keep your fingers spread apart to increase the size of your base of support. With your feet raised off the floor, balance on your hands for five seconds.

Knee-Elbow Handstand

Headstand

(1) Squat with your hands on the mat, shoulder width apart, and extend one leg to the rear. Place your head on the mat in front of your hands to form a triangular base of support for the headstand.

(2) Gently push with your bent leg and raise your extended leg (keeping it straight) over your head. Maintain balance as the toe of the pushing leg leaves the mat.

(3–4) Bring your legs together over your head. Balance on the top of your head so that your body will be perpendicular to the floor.

Headstand

1 2 3 4

A spotter should hold the student's legs until the headstand is learned.

Headstand with Spotter

Forearm Stand

(1) Squat with one leg extended to the rear. Place your forearms on the mat about shoulder width apart. The upper arms should remain vertical.

(2) Carefully raise your kicking leg (extended leg) while pushing off the mat with the bent leg. Place one leg at a time in a vertical position as you fight for balance. Watch the mat between your arms from start to finish, but do not hold your head back too far or your back will arch too much.

(3) Balance by shifting your shoulders slightly forward or backward.

If you allow your upper arms to lean forward too much, you will tip over and begin to fall on your back. If this happens, duck your head and land on your shoulders and upper back as you roll over. Of course, this can be avoided if you have someone support you until you have established control. The spotter stands on the kicking leg side and grasps the leg as the performer pushes off the mat with the other leg. Both legs are then held to keep the performer balanced, and the spotter should make sure that the shoulders are over the elbows and the back is straight. The performer should return to the starting position one leg at a time.

1   2   3

Handstand with Spotter

Now practice the handstand with the aid of a spotter. The spotter stands on
the kicking leg side and catches the leg as it goes up, then grasps the other leg
as it is raised. This technique will help you learn the single-leg kick to the
handstand position safely.

(1) Squat with one leg extended to the rear and place your hands on the mat, shoulder width apart. Spread your fingers and keep your eyes on the mat between your hands.

(2) With your arms straight, practice kicking your rear leg to a near-handstand position. The pushing leg should be straightened and raised but should not be lifted as high as the kicking leg at this point.

(3) If you can execute steps (1) and (2) consistently and with good style, you can now bring your lower leg overhead to join your kicking leg.

Handstand with Spotter

1   2   3

Your spotter should hold your legs overhead, and remind you to keep your eyes focused on the floor, to hold your back straight, and to balance with your shoulders directly over your hands.

The Handstand

Having performed all of the preliminary steps, you are now ready to practice the handstand unaided. This fundamental core skill is considered basic to the advanced performer and *essential* to the intermediate-level performer. The "secret" to learning the handstand is *lots of practice.* Attempt to execute twenty handstands every day if you want to learn it fast.

(1) Squat with your kicking leg extended to the rear. Place your hands on the floor about twelve inches in front of your forward foot and shoulder width apart. Spread your fingers as wide apart as possible to aid balance and keep your eyes on the mat between your hands at all times.

(2–3) Kick your rear leg up to a vertical position by pushing with your front leg until it straightens. You may allow your shoulders to lean forward *slightly* during the kick, but they must be brought back over your hands as the second leg joins the first. If you try to hold a handstand with your shoulders forward, you will topple forward.

(4) Maintain balance by pressing with your fingertips as you feel your body leaning too far forward in an "overbalance." Counter an "underbalance" by quickly bending your elbows slightly and attempting to catch yourself before your body leans too far in the other direction. If you have weak arms, beware of bending them at all; you may collapse.

Handstand

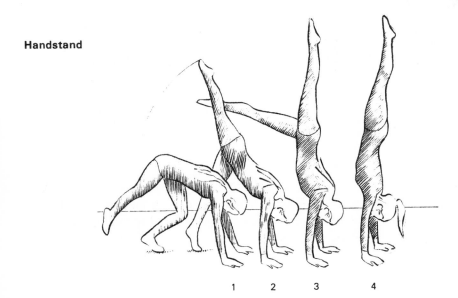

1   2   3   4

Turn-out

If you are confident and experienced enough, you may consider practicing your handstand against a wall or with the back of your head against a bed. If you do not use such support, learn to "turn out" of your handstand when you overbalance by mistake. (Before you practice the turn-out, you must be very efficient at kicking up to a good handstand position.) Have someone spot you the first couple of times or until you acquire a knack for the turn-out. As your handstand starts to overbalance, push with your right hand and quickly place it in front of your left hand (fingers facing left) as you rotate your body, and step down with your right foot. This motion could be called a cartwheel from a handstand. The turn-out described here has a leftward cartwheel motion. If your natural inclination is to perform a cartwheel with your body facing in the other direction, your turn-out should also be in that direction.

It is particularly important to have straight body alignment in the handstand position. You must learn not to thrust your hips outward; otherwise your back will arch. Practice keeping your pelvis "tucked under" while standing erect against a wall and while lying on your back. Learn to assume this straight position while holding a handstand against a wall. Your fingers should almost touch the wall, and you will have to duck your head between your arms to rest on the wall correctly. Push out in the shoulders as much as possible.

2

Floor Exercise: General Information

BRIEF HISTORY

The floor exercise event is simply a planned combination of physical movements without apparatus. It is the oldest event in the sport of gymnastics. Every known society has engaged in ritual dances or acrobatic movements of one kind or another.

During the late nineteenth and early twentieth centuries, many European countries regularly held mass exercise exhibitions. Hundreds of people participated in these routines, which usually took place in large open areas or stadiums. Many of the skills performed today, such as handstands, splits, and arabesques, were incorporated in elaborate combinations of movement. The occasion was usually a national athletics festival that brought young and old athletes together in a demonstration of unity and physical fitness.

As the rules of the sport of gymnastics became more refined, so did the format for the floor exercise event. The gymnast was given a large area in which to perform elaborate dance and tumbling combinations, and eventually a mat replaced the hard wooden floor. Music was added because it

43

helped to create excitement and complemented the gymnast's movements. Music had often been played during mass exhibitions in the open fields, but now it accompanied the performances of individual gymnasts.

Currently, floor exercise is performed to music that has a specified time limit, and is composed of various tumbling, acrobatic, and dance skills combined to form a harmonious whole. Although a competing gymnast's score is primarily based on how well she performs tumbling and acrobatic skills, dance comprises at least half of the routine.

Variety of movement is an important feature of a well-composed floor exercise routine. Skills that move forward, backward, and sideways should be supplemented with twists and elevation changes. The music used should reflect these features as well as the distinctive style and rhythm of the performer. The observer should be impressed by both the total performance and the execution of the separate skills.

FLOOR EXERCISE COMPOSITION

Three of the four Olympic gymnastic events have their own compositional requirement. Although the major requirements change very little over the years, a serious coach or gymnast should have a copy of the latest rules and supplements, available from the United States Gymnastics Federation (U.S.G.F.), P.O. Box 4699, Tucson, Arizona 85717. Very often the International Gymnastics Federation (F.I.G.) makes small additions and deletions on an annual basis.

The following is a general outline of compositional considerations for the floor exercise event.

Floor Exercise Movements

Tumbling
A routine should contain *at least three* tumbling sequences. Variety of direction —forward, backward, and lateral movements—should be included.

Acrobatic Movements

A routine should contain *at least one* such skill. Examples are walkovers, aerials, and the butterfly.

Dance Elements

- Leaps, hops, and jumps should be included in at least two sequences. Demonstrate elevation, flexibility, and variety.
- Turns and pirouettes may be used liberally but not excessively. These elements may be employed to change direction or in moving from one skill into another. Include at least one 360-degree turn or pirouette.
- Poses should be interspersed throughout the routine to emphasize a movement, gain control, and promote the theme of an exercise. Poses are most often used to accent the beginning or end of a musical phrase. The gymnast may also control the rhythm of a sequence by the use of long or short duration poses.
- Low movement, such as rolls or turns on the back, stomach, seat, and knees, should be included to change elevation and add variety to a routine. *At least one* such sequence should be considered.
- Modern dance movements should be featured two or three times in a routine even if they last only a moment. These include walking, running, sliding, body waves, contractions, extensions, and rotations.

In general, a routine should have the following qualities:

- Movement throughout the entire performance area (variety of direction)
- Variety of movement and elevation
- Changes of rhythm
- Harmony of movement and music
- Theme (modern, classical, etc.)
- Organization

Floor Exercise Music

Choosing the music for your floor exercise routine will be one of the more exciting aspects of your gymnastic training. If you have a coach, find out her or his thoughts about the kinds of music best suited to your style and ability.

It is not unusual to see beginning gymnasts trying to perform to music that is entirely inappropriate for them. Many beginners choose their music because they "like it" or want to look like the music sounds (balletic, jazzy, and so on). Although both reasons are important in making a decision, they should be backed up by more objective considerations. Here are some thoughts on this subject:

- If you have had considerable dance training, you may be able to use almost any kind of music.
- If you are a good, fast tumbler, choose music with some fast phrases.
- If you are heavy and slow, you will not want to use light, quick music.
- If you are light and bouncy, you may want to use lively, happy music.
- If your floor exercise style is simple with clear, precise movements, do not choose intricate or jumbled music.
- The short duration of a floor exercise routine usually dictates the use of one melody. The melody chosen should emphasize the best qualities of the gymnast.
- The music should be melodically and rhythmically clear so that the gymnast can easily orient herself after vigorous tumbling sequences in noisy gymnasiums.
- The musical accompaniment should contain contrasting passages so that clear distinctions of movement can be shown. Musical sameness can be boring to an audience in a large, acoustically poor gymnasium.
- The coordination of the gymnast's movements with the music must be clear and unmistakable.
- If you are a beginner, consider ordering a record or tape of floor exercise music from a gymnastics dealer. Most of the commercial records are designed for various levels of ability and have a great deal of variety.

Floor Exercise Poses

Every floor exercise routine contains several poses or momentary hold positions. A great variety of poses can be performed because of the wide range of positions that can be assumed by the human body. One can assume a pose in any position. A good gymnast even tries to pose, for just an instant, while leaping in the air or somersaulting.

When you pose in gymnastics, you are attempting to give the viewer a sustained look at a position that you find very attractive or that helps to create a mood (character pose). An attractive position is not necessarily aesthetic, although that is usually the case. It can be attractive because it requires great flexibility or balance.

Although a character pose is often meant to be attractive, its main function is to help characterize the theme of the exercise. For instance, rounded shoulders and hooked toes are generally considered poor form in classical ballet but may be perfectly in order if your exercise has modern dance or jazz elements. Your character pose may simply be fanciful, if that is what your routine calls for.

When you choose a pose for your exercise, consider how well it harmonizes with the skills performed before and after the pose. Also, keep in mind that the music you choose must allow you to strike the pose on a particular beat or during a pause. One very important function of the momentary hold position is to allow you a moment to rest or regain composure before beginning a particularly arduous task. Many gymnasts purposely perform a slow movement or series of movements prior to a pose to allow even more time to catch their breath for an ensuing difficult tumbling run.

If you are not used to posing, stand in front of a mirror (full length, if possible) and examine the angles of your limbs, the position of your head, and your general posture as you assume the poses in the following illustrations. You will learn very quickly what poses you can do best. Just as your body type and flexibility may dictate, to some extent, the floor exercise routine and style that you pursue, these physical factors may also limit you to certain poses. You do not want to show off something that does not look good on you.

Do not hesitate to devise your own poses to fit your routine. Many gymnasts spend hours rolling on the floor and crawling on their knees, trying to invent special poses for themselves that will fit a particular routine. Very often this process results in unique transitions and artistic hold positions.

Poses

Poses

For purposes of clarity, somersaulting and twisting in gymnastics are described in terms of rotating around three different axes. An axis may be described as an imaginary line on which the body pivots (circles) while rotating during a particular skill.

Sometimes a gymnast circles on more than one axis, particularly during the performance of complicated twisting, somersaulting skills. Knowledge of axes and directions can make teaching and learning various skills a little bit easier. In order to explain this concept, *the center of gravity* must first be defined.

The center of gravity is an imaginary point located in the middle of the body. When you are standing erect it is located slightly below and behind your navel. It is difficult to pinpoint the exact location of one's center of gravity because it varies slightly from one individual to another according to body structure. If you are top-heavy, your center of gravity will be slightly higher than the norm. If you raise your arms over your head, your center of gravity will shift to a slightly higher position. If you jump and touch your toes in a piked position, your center of gravity moves forward (outside the body) to a point in the middle of your pike.

The more your mass is concentrated around your center of gravity, the faster you will rotate or twist. The body rotates faster in a tucked position than in a layout during the performance of a somersault. Bringing your arms close to your body while twisting speeds up the twist.

Like the hub of a spinning wheel, the center point of the three axes of the body is its center of gravity. When you somersault forward or backward, you are rotating on a lateral axis that extends through the approximate center of your body from side to side. When you somersault sideways, you are rotating on a front-to-back axis that passes through your stomach to your backbone. The axis around which your body rotates during a twisting movement is called a longitudinal axis because it runs vertically from the middle of your head to between your feet.

How do you determine the direction in which you are moving? Gymnastics experts at the turn of the century made it very easy for us. They decided that all directions would be determined on the basis of an image that has the gymnast standing next to the face of a clock. This approach took into consideration all three axes of rotation.

In the illustration, the performer is jumping into a forward somersault with the face of a clock on her left side. She is rotating clockwise. If she were to execute a somersault counter-clockwise, she would be performing a backward somersault.

Direction of twist is always determined with the face of a clock facing you at your feet. The illustration demonstrates a right, or clockwise, twist. If the performer were to twist counter-clockwise, she would be twisting left.

When you turn over in a sideways plane, as in a cartwheel, the direction of rotation is always determined by the face of a clock facing you. Counter-clockwise movement is a left rotation, and a clockwise motion is a right rotation.

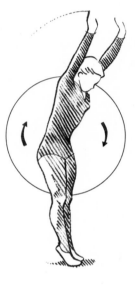

Clockwise Somersault

Counter-clockwise Cartwheel

Clockwise Twist

When determining direction of movement, it is important to keep in mind that the face of the clock must always be visualized in the positions described and illustrated here. This is particularly important in determining the direction of a twist. For instance, when you perform a *round-off* or any other twisting skill, you may bend down and partially rotate on a left-sideways axis (left hand is placed on the mat first), but you actually *twist* a half turn to the right. The rule here is that when you are oriented in an inverted position (face of the clock at your feet), it always seems as though you are twisting in a direction that is contrary to the fact. Thus, if you wish to continue twisting in the same direction while performing any skill that has a left round-off action (right twist), you must perform the ensuing twist to the right.

3

Floor Exercise Skills: Tumbling and Acrobatics

Although they are usually considered separate categories, tumbling and acrobatic skills are discussed together here because most coaches combine both kinds of movements in their teaching. However, the distinction between the two should be indicated.

Tumbling skills are explosively fast movements linked together and usually performed in a straight line. Each component of a tumbling sequence is a "building block" that powers the next skill. Tumbling movements are characterized by "free flight" and agility.

Acrobatic skills usually involve flexibility and slower-moving balance techniques. These skills do not usually set one up for powerful recoveries. Although there are exceptions, acrobatic skills generally do not require springing into the air from the mat. However, some acrobatic movements are also considered tumbling skills.

In the discussions of the floor exercise skills that follow, of particular interest are the variations described. Such modifications are usually the result of imaginative experimentation. Once having learned a basic skill pattern, every gymnast has the right to alter the classical model within the framework of the current acceptable competitive rules and trends.

FORWARD ROLL

Skill Level 1

Rolling skills are important building blocks in the sport of gymnastics. Every beginner should learn a number of variations of rolling skills because they are related to many sophisticated, advanced skills in every event. Learn the forward roll first. The beginner should start from a full squat position.

Basic Description

(1–4) Squat with knees together and place hands on the mat about ten inches in front of knees. (The illustration shows a somewhat advanced version of the forward roll in that the performer assumes only a partial squat.) Push with both legs until they straighten, and bend arms in order to lower the back of the head on the mat.

(5–6) Bring legs into a tuck position, grasp knees, and roll forward to feet.

(7–8) Continue rolling forward to a squat and stand up.

Forward Roll

1   2   3   4

5   6   7   8

After practicing several forward rolls and attaining a smooth rolling action, begin squatting less and jumping a little as you start the roll. Always bend your arms to absorb the shock as your hands hit the mat, and do not duck your head under until it is about to contact the mat. If you land heavily on your back, you are probably ducking your head early and/or not lowering your body smoothly by bending your arms.

Prerequisite
Ability to roll backward from a squat position onto your back until your head touches the mat, and then roll forward in a tucked position and up to your feet.

Spotting
Hold the performer's waist or hips with both hands and guide the upper back onto the mat as the head is ducked. Lift to remove some of the weight from the performer's arms and head.

Forward Roll Spotting

Once you have mastered the basic forward roll technique, you are ready to practice several variations of this roll. Follow the illustrations carefully. The variations are presented in their approximate order of difficulty.

Step into Forward Roll (Variation)

Skill Level 1

Take a big step forward, bend the front knee, and push off with the forward leg. Bring your legs together as you roll over. If the forward roll is part of a tumbling sequence, your body position as you stand up after the roll will vary to suit the skill that follows.

Step into Forward Roll

Straddle Stand to Forward Roll to Step-out (Variation)

Skill Level 1

Notice that the gymnast in the illustration has modified the placement of the hands on the mat. She has put her hands, fingers facing backward, between her feet. Also notice that she ends up in a squat position with one leg forward, called a *step-out*.

Straddle Stand to Forward Roll to Step-out

Sit and Turn to Forward Roll (Variation)
Skill Level 2

From a sitting position, turn in a continuous motion as you push off the mat into a forward roll. This action requires lots of leg thrust to elevate the hips for a smooth roll.

Sit and Turn to Forward Roll

Arched Dive Forward Roll (Variation)

Skill Level 4

The most advanced form of the forward roll is the dive roll. The ability to remain in the air long enough to assume the arched position depends on a fast run and strong legs. Always use a crash mat (a soft, twelve-inch-thick mat) while learning this skill. Note that as you descend toward the mat your body must rotate just enough to allow you to briefly assume a near-handstand position before bending your arms to roll smoothly over. A good spotter is recommended.

Basic Description

(1–3) Execute a fast run and jump, pushing off with both feet. Jump forward with a vigorous lift of the arms. Your knees should not bend very much prior to the takeoff.

(4–5) Arch your back by bringing your heels up in the rear. Your upper body should not lower as you arch. Assume an arched position at the peak of the jump. Reach for the mat with arms extended well before contact is made. Watch the mat until your arms bend slightly upon landing.

(6–8) As contact is made, bend elbows and hips to absorb the shock, and roll to your feet.

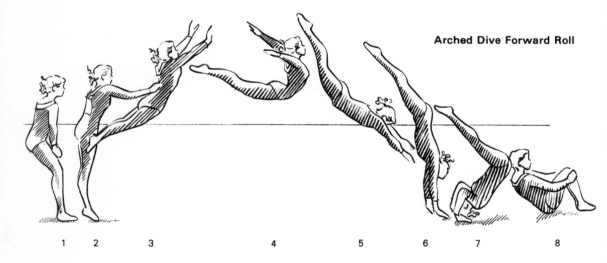

Arched Dive Forward Roll

1   2   3   4   5   6   7   8

If you have trouble learning how to arch immediately after jumping, try some arched jumps using a spotting belt attached to overhead ropes.

Prerequisites

Jump to forward roll and handstand to forward roll.

Spotting

Stand on the right side of the performer just in front of the crash mat. As performer jumps, catch and support her below the rib cage with right forearm and hand. At the same time, bring your left forearm and hand under the thighs, grasp the legs, and regulate the amount of rotation. Release performer when she is safely on her back.

BACKWARD ROLL TO ONE KNEE

Skill Level 1

This roll may also be done in a tucked position all the way over to both knees or to a step-out. Most beginners find it difficult to get both hands flat on the mat under the shoulders early enough to protect the head as the roll is executed. If you have this problem, practice rolling backward and putting your hands under your shoulders without rolling all the way over. Roll backward quickly in order to get your hips over your head efficiently.

Basic Description

(1–4) Squat to a sit in a tight tucked position, bring hands up and behind you, roll backward, and bring knees overhead. Move your arms into position to reach backward under your shoulders.

(5) Quickly place hands on mat under shoulders. Push with your arms (keep weight off head) as your legs pass over your head. Separate legs and lower right knee toward the mat.

(6) Continue pushing with arms as weight is transferred to right leg.

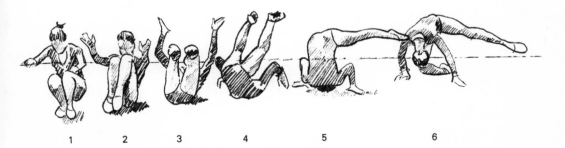

1   2   3   4   5   6

Backward Roll to One Knee

Prerequisite

Ability to roll backward from a squat and place hands under shoulders before head touches the mat.

Spotting

Assist the performer from the side by holding the hips as they pass over the head. The spotter should remove some of the weight on the head (assist the arm push) by gently lifting the performer's hips over her head in a slow movement. Repeat until the motion becomes continuous.

Backward Roll Spotting

Backward Shoulder Roll to One Knee (Variation)

Skill Level 1

This roll provides a much smoother rolling action than the straight backward roll. Notice that as the roll occurs the head is turned under the supporting right arm, eliminating pressure on the head. See Chapter 5 for an illustration of the use of this roll in a sequence.

Basic Description

(1–3) Roll backward with legs straight and extend left arm to the side, palm down.

(4–6) Separate legs (left leg leads), bend left knee, and roll over on left shoulder. Head is turned to the side and right arm is used to push. Place left knee on mat.

(7–8) Push with hands and straighten up, with right leg extended to the side.

Backward Shoulder Roll to One Knee

Backward Shoulder Roll to Chest Roll (Variation)

Skill Level 2

Practice this roll on an extra-soft mat until you have mastered the vertical leg thrust and the arching technique. Learn it from a sitting position before adding the fancy modifications depicted in the illustration.

Basic Description

(1–5) Roll backward with arms out to the sides.

(6–7) Extend right arm on the mat, palm down, and shoot legs upward over

64

right shoulder. At the same time, place left hand under left shoulder and turn head to the side so that it does not bear weight.

(8–10) Arch your back and lower first your chest and then your legs to the mat. Use your bent support arm to help you control the descent of your body toward the mat. Keep your back arched throughout or you may land heavily on your knees.

Backward Shoulder Roll to Chest Roll

Spotting
Hold the performer's legs up as she extends her hips, and carefully lower her into the chest roll.

Backward Roll Shoot to Handstand (Variation)
Skill Level 4

Learn this skill with your legs together before attempting the illustrated version.

Basic Description
(1–4) Execute a fast, smooth, sitting-backward rolling action with an early placement of the hands under the shoulders.

(5–8) Shoot legs upward and push with arms very hard. The type of handstand you perform depends on your preference and ability. The illustration depicts a single-leg squat and roll followed by a leg shoot to a rather striking pose before the final split handstand.

Spotting
Lift legs (holding feet together) to support performer as shoot occurs.

Backward Roll Shoot to Handstand

SKIP STEP (HURDLE)

Skill Level 1

Learning to hurdle correctly is very important because this skill precedes forward handsprings, round-offs, and aerial skills.

The basic hurdle is a simple skip step that most children learn while playing various games. The movement has two phases:

Ascending: Step forward on one foot and hop while lifting the knee of the other leg toward the stomach.

Descending: Land on hopping foot and step forward with the other foot.

This action may be practiced in a series by stepping forward with the hopping foot and repeating the movement many times: step-hop-step, step-hop-step, and so on.

An important point to be kept in mind by the beginning performer is that most gymnasts perform the hop of the skip step with the foot of the leg they naturally use to kick into handstands, cartwheels, round-offs, and handsprings. Your most efficient kicking leg in performing the handstand—the leg that "feels the best"—is also the leg you should use for the hop of the skip step.

There is a very limited advantage in learning the hurdle equally well with either foot, although compulsory exercise routines sometimes require performers to execute skills on their "bad side." Use the same leg for hopping (in the hurdle) and kicking (in cartwheels and handsprings) all the time for consistency.

Whether you perform the skip step "high" or "long" is determined by the kind of skill that follows it. A high-leaping skip step is inappropriate if its objective is to set you up for a long, low round-off and backward handspring series. On the other hand, a high hop could be advantageous prior to executing an aerial cartwheel because aerial skills are best performed high and short. However, the sport of gymnastics is not an exact science and therefore leaves much room for individual preference in this and other matters.

There are two basic styles of the skip step.

Bent-Knee Skip Step

Skill Level 1

The bent-knee skip step is not considered as aesthetically appealing as the straight-leg variety. However, many top-flight gymnasts use this style for difficult backward tumbling sequences because it puts them in a better position for the movement that follows.

Bent-Knee Skip Step

Straight-Leg Skip Step

Skill Level 1

The straight-leg skip step is often used to perform an attractive hop prior to forward handsprings and aerial somersaults where a pushing-backward (blocking) action against the mat occurs. In this case, the straight-leg style looks better and also often provides a desirable body angle for takeoff. Learn the basic bent-knee style of skip step before the straight-leg version. The bent-knee style is easier and functions well for everyone.

Straight-Leg Skip Step

CARTWHEEL

Skill Level 2

The cartwheel, like the handstand, is a core skill of gymnastics. It should be performed with a smooth, continuous motion.

Basic Description

(1–2) Stand sideways or forward with arms overhead. Step forward with either foot. (Choose your best side.) Lean forward and bend front knee as foot touches mat.

(3–4) Place hands sideways (fingers pointing to the left if left foot is forward) on mat one at a time and push with bent forward leg as you kick other leg over your head. Keep head tilted back slightly so that you can watch the mat as you rotate.

(5) Pass through a handstand sideways with legs spread as much as possible. Remain extended in the shoulders and lower back throughout.

(6–9) Place leading foot on mat about six inches from the nearest hand, raise upper body, and bring the other leg to the mat.

Cartwheel

1 2 3 4 5 6 7 8 9

Prerequisite
Ability to kick to a handstand (though holding this position is unnecessary).

Spotting
(1) Stand on the side that the performer will lead with to begin the cartwheel, and place your near hand against performer's waist, palm up.
(2) As performer leans toward the mat, grip her waist while reaching across her back with other hand to grasp her waist on the other side.

Lift and guide the performer through the handstand position and the landing.

Cartwheel Spotting

1   2

Far-Arm One-Arm Cartwheel (Variation)
Skill Level 3

Review the technique and spotting instructions for the basic cartwheel. This variation may be performed with either arm. Try to learn it both ways. Your kick must be faster for a one-arm cartwheel than for a regular cartwheel. Keep your shoulder over your supporting hand as you pass through the handstand position.

Far-Arm One-Arm Cartwheel

Dive Cartwheel (Variation)

Skill Level 3

Basic Description

(1) Perform a skip step with arms extended rearward behind hips.

(2–4) Push off the mat with bent (forward) leg and extend arms forward. Attempt to gain as much elevation as possible in the jump before descending, but only after you have gradually increased the height of the jump in successive attempts.

(5–8) Place hands on mat one at a time and keep legs straight and as wide apart as possible throughout the rotation.

1   2   3   4   5

Dive Cartwheel

6   7   8

ROUND-OFF

Skill Level 2

The round-off is often used as a lead-in to skills such as the backward hand-spring and backward somersault. It should be done as aggressively as a forward handspring. Learn to perform a strong round-off from one step as well as from a running skip step.

Basic Description

(1–3) Execute a skip step. Step forward twenty-four inches, bend forward knee, and place hands on mat one at a time with fingers facing sideways. The start of the round-off is very similar to that of the cartwheel; however, the second hand to be placed on the mat turns slightly more at the wrist and reaches a little farther to the side. Kick rear leg over your head as first hand touches the mat (as with basic cartwheel).

(4–7) Continue onto other hand as legs are brought closer together, and make an additional quarter turn as legs join for the landing. During this phase, the shoulders should be extended as you push off the mat to accelerate their movement upward in preparation for the landing. Push with both arms simultaneously as the second hand contacts the mat.

Round-off

1   2   3   4

Prerequisites

Cartwheel and skip step.

Spotting

Refer to the spotting instructions for the cartwheel. Assist the performer further by guiding the hips (pulling them toward you) during the last phase if necessary.

TINSICA

Skill Level 4

The tinsica may be executed with a diving action similar to that of the dive cartwheel. It is a combination cartwheel and forward walkover (discussed later). As you become more familiar with this skill through repetition, it will begin to feel like a walkover with your hands staggered.

5 6 7

Basic Description

(1–2) Start in the position assumed for a cartwheel (sideways or forward) and begin as you would start a cartwheel, except that the hands are placed on the mat (one at a time) with the *fingers facing forward*.

(3–5) As your weight is transferred to the forward arm, the hip is turned forward. To facilitate moving into the final, standing position, the back must be arched considerably to get the lead foot on the mat as close to the forward hand as possible.

(6–7) The shoulder of the lead arm must be fully extended as the stand occurs. Continue arching your back and keep your head back as you move into the standing position.

Tinsica

1   2   3

4   5   6   7

Prerequisites

Cartwheel and ability to stand up from a bridge position.

Spotting

Spotting is the same as for the cartwheel in the beginning, but the hips must be guided outward in the last phase. Spot the performer under the lower back as she moves into the stand.

HEADSPRING

Skill Level 4

When you do a headspring, try to be as dynamic and forceful as possible with your arm-pushing action so that you do not have to rely on excessive arching to land on your feet.

Basic Description

(1–2) Squat with legs together and place your head on the mat between hands. (You may also step into the headspring position.) Push with legs and pike hips sharply.

  (3) Bring hips over and beyond the head, creating a slight overbalance. Start slowly! After several successful repetitions, increase the speed as you move into the piked position.

  (4) Extend the hips, arch your back, and whip legs around while pushing hard with your arms. Extend the arms and shoulders fully.

  (5) In landing, try to bring your feet down as close as possible to where your hands were. Maintain an arch with your head held back until you are balanced on your feet.

Headspring

1   2   3   4   5

Prerequisites

Headstand and bridge position.

Spotting

Stand to the right of the performer. Grasp her right upper arm with your left hand as she places her head on the mat. Place your right forearm on her lower back and gently pull her into an overbalance with her hips leading. As the leg shoot occurs, support the lower back and maintain your hold on the upper arm to prevent it from hitting you. Guide the performer to a stand.

Headspring to Step-out (Variation)

Skill Level 4

In this version of the headspring, as you land bring your lead foot under your hips as far as possible in order to step out with a smooth forward motion.

Headspring to Step-out

Headspring to Straddle Seat (Variation)

Skill Level 4

Overbalance slightly more than is required for a regular headspring. Land on your heels with your hips off the mat and bend forward quickly to soften the landing.

Headspring to Straddle Seat

FORWARD WALKOVER

Skill Level 4

Perform the forward walkover in a smooth, continuous movement.

Basic Description

    (1) Stand with arms extended over your head. Raise one leg and step forward.

(2–3) Place hands on floor about twelve inches in front of foot. The front knee may be slightly bent.

(4–5) Kick through handstand position and keep head up so that you can watch the mat. Split legs as much as possible.

    (6) Stretch shoulders upward as you place your lead foot on the mat as close to your hands as possible. Do not allow your shoulders to sag forward.

(7–9) Transfer body weight from hands to lead leg. Keep your head back and arch as much as possible as you straighten to a stand.

Forward Walkover

1   2   3   4   5   6

7   8   9

Prerequisites

At least some control in handstand position. Ability to stand up from a bridge and from a handstand arch over to both feet.

Spotting

Place hand or forearm on performer's lower back and the other hand above the knee as she kicks to a handstand.

Forward Walkover Spotting

Support the performer and encourage a smooth motion by shifting your arm to her shoulders and gently pressing them as she overbalances. Carefully guide performer as she rotates, grasping her upper arm as she lands and rises to a one-foot stand and helping to transfer the body weight from the arms to the legs.

One-Arm Forward Walkover (Variation)

Skill Level 5

The one-arm forward walkover should be performed slightly faster than a two-arm forward walkover because maintaining balance is more difficult with one arm than with two. Keep the shoulder of your support arm over your hand as you pass through the handstand position.

One-Arm Forward Walkover

From Knee: Forward Walkover to Split (Variation)

Skill Level 5

Practice kicking to a split handstand from one knee before attempting this variation. As you land, attempt to gain support with the instep of your lead foot before removing your hands from the mat.

From Knee: Forward Walkover to Split

Dive Forward Walkover (Variation)

Skill Level 6

Use a skip step approach and a strong outward stretching of your arms on takeoff. Split your legs wider after you land on your hands to aid forward rotation.

Dive Forward Walkover

Jump Half Turn to Forward Walkover (Variation)

Skill Level 7

This skill is usually executed from a round-off or backward handspring. The performer must hold arms over her head during the jump turn to keep her body from moving sideways. Notice also that the handstand landing is under-balanced to compensate for a great deal of forward rotation.

Jump Half Turn to Forward Walkover

BACKWARD WALKOVER

Skill Level 4

Like the forward walkover, this skill should be executed in a smooth, continuous movement.

Basic Description

(1) Stand with arms over your head and weight on one leg. The forward leg may be either raised or placed slightly in front of support leg. Stretch upward through stomach and chest to arch upper back area.

(2–3) Arch backward with weight on support leg. Place hands on the mat as close to support leg as possible. Try to hold your head back far enough to be able to see the support leg as hands touch the mat.

(4–6) Push off with slightly bent support leg at the moment hands touch the mat, and kick forward leg over your head. Split legs as much as possible throughout. Do not let shoulders sag forward as body passes through handstand. Extend shoulders to the maximum.

(7–8) Place lead leg on the mat close to hands and stand with rear leg held as high as possible.

1   2   3   4   5

Backward Walkover

Prerequisites

Control in handstand position. Ability to lower to and stand up from a bridge, and to perform handstand arch over to bridge and stand.

Spotting

Stand beside performer next to her forward leg. Place one hand on lower back and guide performer into position as she leans backward. Place other hand under thigh of forward (kicking) leg and gently push leg over performer's head during the kick-over. Shift your hand from the kicking leg to stomach area and your other hand from the lower back to rearward (high) leg and continue to aid rotation as performer descends from handstand to the landing.

6 7 8

Backward Walkover and Switch Legs (Variation)

Skill Level 4

This skill requires slightly more leg push than a regular backward walkover. Note that the lead leg becomes the rearward or following leg after it is passed by the other leg as you pass through the handstand position. Assume maximum split position after leg switch occurs.

Backward Walkover and Switch Legs

Backward Walkover to Straddle-down (Variation)

Skill Level 5

This skill requires a delicate sense of balance in the handstand position. Keep your hips directly over your head as you spread your legs as wide as possible before lowering your body to a straddle support position with your seat and legs off the mat.

Backward Walkover to Straddle-down

Valdez (Variation)

Skill Level 4

The valdez begins in a sitting position and ends in a handstand. Numerous variations are possible in the performance of this skill, giving the gymnast the opportunity to display her personal style. Illustrated here is the valdez to a step-out.

Basic Description

(1) Sit on the mat with right knee raised and left leg extended forward. Place your right hand about four inches behind your right hip, with fingers facing rearward.

(2–6) Push with your bent right leg until it straightens, while throwing your left leg directly overhead and reaching back toward the mat with your left arm. If you intend to finish in the handstand position rather than continue rotation to a step-out, turn your supporting right hand to the same position as the other hand's as you go into the handstand; if you

1   2   3   4   5

Valdez

step out as illustrated, it is not necessary to change the position of the right hand on the mat.

(7) Notice that the kicking leg moves right past the handstand if you choose to step out.

(8) As you step out, keep right leg straight.

Beginners with flexible backs often find it easier to reach backward to a bridge and kick over in a backward walkover movement.

Prerequisites
Some control during handstand. Ability to lower to and stand up from a bridge.

Spotting
Squat on one knee on performer's kicking leg side. Place one hand on performer's lower back and one hand under thigh. As the skill is initiated, assist the kicking leg and support the lower back. Continue assistance until performer reaches handstand position.

6　　　　　7　　　　　　　8

Half Turn from Knees to Backward Walkover (Variation)
Skill Level 5

Using one arm for support, turn and push with the toes of one foot, extending the toes as much as possible. Reach high with the kicking leg, and split legs to the maximum.

Half Turn from Knees to Backward Walkover

Backward Walkover to Forward Walkover (Variation)
Skill Level 7

The left hand is brought down on the mat with the wrist turned inward (facing the head). This wrist position allows the performer to execute a backward pirouette turn to a handstand and then move into a forward walkover.

FORWARD HANDSPRING

Skill Level 5

The length of your step after the hop and the extent to which you stretch forward to place your hands on the mat are determined by the speed of your steps into the handspring. A fast run dictates a larger step and farther reach.

Basic Description

(1–4) Execute skip step after one or two preliminary steps. Step forward, bend knee, and place hands on the mat in front of lead foot. Kick rear leg over your head as you push off by extending bent front leg. This should be a very forceful kick.

  (5) Extend shoulders upward and straighten arms (if they are bent) as body passes through handstand. Watch the mat between your hands as long as possible after kicking to the handstand.

(6–7) Bring legs together and arch over into a stand.

Forward Handspring

Prerequisites

Hard kick to handstand. Fall over from handstand to bridge and stand.

Spotting

The spot is similar to that of a forward walkover or a headspring. However, the handspring is a much faster movement and requires a more aggressive spotting technique. The spotter must move in quickly, and do a considerable amount of lifting to insure a safe landing. Standing on the right side of the performer, grasp her right upper arm with your left hand as her hands touch the mat and support her lower back with your right arm. Continue assistance until performer has landed.

Forward Handspring to Step-out (Variation)

Skill Level 5

Execute the forward handspring to a step-out by reaching for the mat with your kicking leg throughout rotation until the landing. As the first foot lands, your back should be arched and your head held backward.

Forward Handspring to Step-out

Dive to Forward Handspring to Step-out (Variation)

Skill Level 6

Run and jump from both feet and with your arms held over your head. As you land on your hands, bend hips slightly and immediately push against the mat as your legs split for the step-out.

Dive to Forward Handspring to Step-out

HANDSTAND SNAP-DOWN

Skill Level 3

This skill can also be considered a drill to improve backward tumbling technique. It is the last half of a backward handspring and is often its weakest component when performed by inexperienced gymnasts. The idea is to kick to a near-handstand, arch your back, bend your knees, and snap out of that position to your feet as vigorously as possible. This movement requires quite a bit of coordination and strength, and beginners often end up on their hands and knees.

If you practice this skill to improve your ability to do a series of backward handsprings, in landing try to bring your feet down on the mat in front of your hips and about twelve inches from where your hands were. That leaves you in a piked position with a backward lean—an excellent position from which to launch into the next backward handspring. On the other hand, if you are practicing the best position from which to go into a tucked backward somersault, you should snap down so that you land with your shoulders high, as illustrated.

This skill is important enough to practice every day.

Basic Description

(1) Kick to a near-handstand position. Bend elbows slightly, lean forward with shoulders, arch back, and bend knees.

(2–3) Quickly straighten legs before pushing with arms and snapping legs downward toward the mat in a piking action. This should be done in a fast, continuous movement, the legs moving in a semicircle to the mat.

(4–6) Immediately after landing, jump with a springing action from the ankles, knees, and hips if you are practicing the handstand snap-down as a lead-in to a somersault. Your arms should be brought directly from the mat to the upward thrust position. Then descend to the mat without attempting the somersault.

Handstand Snap-down

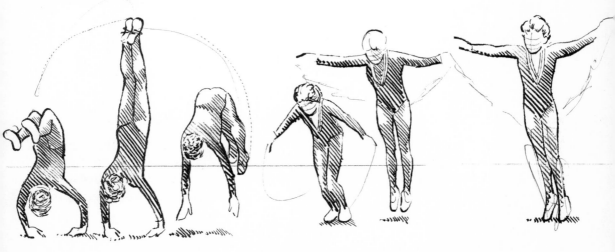

1   2   3   4   5   6

BACKWARD HANDSPRING

Skill Level 5

The power of the backward handspring comes from a sustained leg push. Most beginners mistakenly lift their feet off the mat too soon in an effort to begin body rotation immediately. Practice the handstand snap-down while you are learning the backward handspring.

Basic Description

(1–3) Stand with arms extended straight behind your back. Bend knees ninety degrees and vigorously swing arms (keeping them straight) down and then up overhead in a continuous, circular motion. Do not throw your head back until your arms reach shoulder level. Lean backward and push forcefully with your legs *throughout* this first phase.

(4) Stretch shoulders and arms to the maximum as you reach for the mat. Place your hands on the mat almost directly below your hips, and arch your back.

(5–6) The shoulders usually slump slightly under the weight of the body as hands contact the mat. Push away from the mat by re-extending the shoulders and piking down hard.

1   2   3   4   5   6

Backward Handspring

Prerequisites

Fairly controlled handstand. Handstand snap-down. Experience in most forward springing skills.

Spotting

When the performer is as heavy as the spotter, an additional spotter is recommended. When you spot a backward handspring, be sure of your ability to guide and support the performer throughout the skill.

As the performer bends her knees and prepares to jump backward, place one hand (palm up) and forearm across her lower back, and your other hand on the far upper leg just below the seat. Support the performer as she jumps backward to her hands so that the wrists are not jarred. Push the legs over through a handstand after hands touch the mat.

Backward Handspring Spotting

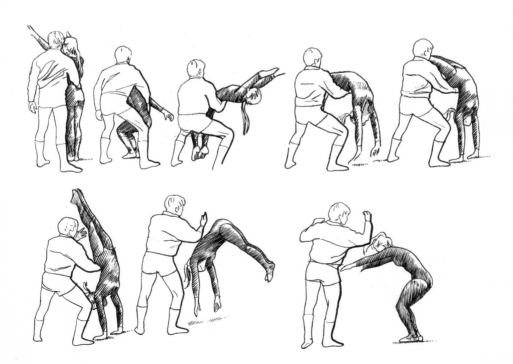

Backward Handspring to Step-out (Variation)
Skill Level 5

The step-out is used when the performer wishes to step into a movement that follows the backward handspring. The legs may be split just before the hands touch the mat or very soon afterward.

Backward Handspring to Step-out

ROUND-OFF TO BACKWARD HANDSPRING
Skill Level 6

This is a power combination of skills usually performed prior to a backward somersault. The transition from round-off to handspring should be executed low and without pause, and power should increase as the sequence proceeds.

When you are learning this combination, it may be helpful to watch your feet for an instant as you land from the round-off.

Basic Description

(1–6) Execute a round-off, bringing your legs slightly farther around than usual so that you land with your feet slightly in front of the hips. Usually, landing in this position would result in a fall to the seat if nothing followed the landing on the round-off, but here it tilts your body slightly backward, giving you a "head start" for the handspring.

(7–12) As the feet are brought down on the mat, the knees bend slightly in preparation for a strong, sustained push, and the arms are thrown overhead as the backward handspring begins. Arch your back well.

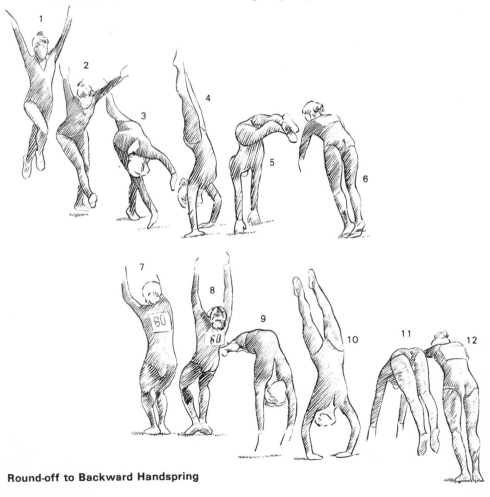

Round-off to Backward Handspring

Prerequisites
Round-off and backward handspring.

Spotting
The first few attempts to perform this combination must be very carefully spotted. The spotter must be able to move with the performer and quickly place a hand on the lower back for support. Both performer and spotter may find it helpful in the beginning to pause briefly after the round-off. The spotter should not hesitate to ask a performer to relearn a particular technique if he notices a weakness in her performance of the combined round-off and backward handspring. If the performer balks after what seems to be a good round-off, it may be because she is throwing her head back before her feet land at the end of the round-off. The spotter or coach should teach the gymnast to keep her head in the natural position as she throws her arms up to begin the backward handspring. The head may be tilted back (so that the mat can be seen) just before the hands contact the mat.

Cartwheel to Backward Handspring to Step-out (Variation)
Skill Level 6

As the rear foot touches the mat after the cartwheel, jump backwards, pushing off with both legs simultaneously. Your objective is to jump as high as possible, so do not lean back too much as you jump.

Cartwheel to Backward Handspring to Step-out

Cartwheel to Backward Dive to Chest Roll (Variation)

Skill Level 7

Place your feet together as you step out of the cartwheel and jump to a high backward dive. Allow your legs to lag behind and arch your back substantially. As your hands touch the mat, bend your arms and smoothly lower your chest and then your legs to the mat.

Cartwheel to Backward Dive to Chest Roll

BUTTERFLY (RIGHT SIDE)

Skill Level 4

The butterfly is often performed in a series of two or more. It is one of the few acrobatic skills that move in a slightly circular pattern rather than in a straight line. The beginning performer must learn to follow through with the initial leg kick until the hip is extended. Keep your eyes on the mat at all times.

Basic Description

(1) Stand with legs spread about three feet apart. Raise both arms and hold them toward the left, or assume the arm position illustrated.

(2–3) Swing right arm downward and bend forward at the hips; the bend increases as you move to the right. The bend of the right leg also increases as the upper body moves right.

(4–5) As the upper body passes over the bent right knee (do not be off-balance because of a too-far-forward lean), push hard with your right leg and throw your left leg and side upward. At this point, your upper body is being pulled to the right and your kicking leg is slightly trailing.

(6–7) Bring your right leg upward so that for a moment you are in a straddled, arched position with your upper body parallel with the floor.

(8–9) Land on your left leg in position for a possible repetition of the butterfly.

Butterfly

1   2   3   4

Prerequisites
Tour jeté (see Chapter 4). Cartwheel.

Spotting
Spotting this skill is very difficult because the performer turns into the spotter and may even kick the spotter. Try holding the performer's hands for support during a few modified attempts.

Cartwheel to Butterfly (Variation)

Skill Level 4

Place your left foot close to your left hand and maintain balance as you step out of the cartwheel. As your right leg steps into position prior to throwing your body into the butterfly, you should have begun the bending movement to the right. Most beginners start bending too late, causing a nose dive.

Cartwheel to Butterfly

AERIAL CARTWHEEL

Skill Level 5

The aerial cartwheel differs from the butterfly in that the kicking leg is brought directly "over the top," whereas in the butterfly the legs are extended somewhat laterally during flight. As you rotate you may bring your arms up past your hips (as illustrated) or hold them down and outward (see aerial forward walk-over). Both types of arm lift are very effective when coordinated with the leg push.

Basic Description

(1–4) Execute a skip step (hurdle). Be sure that your lead foot is placed far enough forward to allow you to be balanced as you push off the mat and go into the cartwheel. The arms swing upward as the hop of the hurdle is executed, then are held with their undersides facing upward as the takeoff occurs. Just before pushing off, the forward leg should be bent almost ninety degrees, and the stomach should be very close to the thigh.

(5–9) Push with the front leg and kick the rear leg over your head as quickly as possible. At the same time, lift upward with arms and shoulders. The arm lift must be carefully coordinated with the leg push to give you sufficient lifting power; however, a strong leg push and kick are the most important considerations here. Split legs as much as possible. Keep your eyes on the mat at all times.

(10–12) Place kicking leg on the mat under the hips as you land. Most beginners do not pull this leg around far enough for the stand.

Prerequisites

Forward handspring to a step-out. Cartwheel. Far- or near-arm one-arm cartwheel with very little weight on support arm.

Spotting

See the spotting instructions for the cartwheel. If performer is executing the aerial cartwheel to her left, stand on her left side. Place your right hand (palm up) on her stomach as she bends forward. Reach over her back with your left hand and grasp her waist on the far side. Carry the performer over to her feet as her weight shifts from your right arm to your left arm.

1   2   3   4   5   6

7   8   9   10

11   12

Aerial Forward Walkover

AERIAL FORWARD WALKOVER
Skill Level 6

Attempt to watch the mat below you throughout the aerial walkover. The arms are held down and outward at first, then rise sharply as the leg push occurs.

Basic Description
(1–3) Execute a skip step as it is done for the aerial cartwheel. The arm action during the initial phase is the same for both skills.

(4–6) Split legs wide and attempt to watch the mat as long as possible. If you are very flexible in the lower back area, try to see the foot of your kicking leg land on the mat.

(7–9) Your lead foot should be placed well under your hip upon landing. This will help insure a secure standing position. Continue thrusting your hips forward and arching as you rise to an erect position.

Prerequisites
Forward handspring to a step-out. One-arm forward handspring to a step-out. Forward walkover. In general, you should be flexible enough to execute a forward walkover and strong enough to do a forward handspring.

Spotting

The performer should throw her arms downward so that the spotter can place a hand on her stomach early in the skill. A forward arm-lifting action will interfere with the spot.

Stand to the left of the performer. Place your right hand on stomach-hip area as performer lowers before pushing off the mat. Lift the performer during the pushing phase with the right hand and place your left hand on her lower back. Support the arch-over and landing with your left hand. Consider using a spotting belt for maximum safety and efficiency.

Aerial Forward Walkover Spotting

Tucked Forward Somersault to Step-out

TUCKED FORWARD SOMERSAULT TO STEP-OUT
Skill Level 7

Learn this skill on a crash mat and land on both feet before attempting to step out. Practice *standing* front somersaults (somersaults without a preliminary run) from a vaulting board onto a crash mat until you can land in a sitting tucked position every time (on your feet would be better). *Be sure to keep your knees well apart when you land in the sitting tucked position to avoid a collision of your knees and face.*

Basic Description

(1–4) Run and execute a skip step, leaping from one foot to a landing on both feet. This should be a short, low leap. Lift and extend arms forward. Your knees should be only slightly bent as you jump so that you can extend quickly at the moment of takeoff.

(5–9) Raise your hips over your shoulders as you curl your back and hunch your shoulders forward. Tuck your chin down to your breastbone and assume a tight tucked position as soon as possible.

(10–11) As you approach the mat, release the tuck, quickly reach under your hips with your landing leg, and step out.

7   8   9

10   11

Prerequisites

Dive roll. Standing front somersault into crash mat. Forward somersault on trampoline, or in a spotting belt. Forward headspring and handspring.

Spotting

Before being hand-spotted, the performer should be given some forward somersault training, preferably on a trampoline while wearing a spotting belt with overhead rigging. When hand-spotting, use the spotting technique for a forward handspring to piked forward somersault. Spot the forward somersault with a

Tucked Forward Somersault to Step-out Spotting

twelve-inch-thick crash mat under the performer for the landing. As she gains confidence in the spot, use less matting.

Stand to the left of the performer. As the takeoff occurs, place your right hand (palm up) and forearm below her rib cage, and reach across her back with your left hand. Lift with right arm as performer jumps, then support and rotate her with both hands. Spotting this skill requires considerable effort, so be prepared.

FORWARD HANDSPRING TO PIKED FORWARD SOMERSAULT TO STEP-OUT
Skill Level 10

The piked somersault requires additional handspring power. Learn a forward handspring to a tucked forward somersault before working on the piked somersault. With both, it is a good idea to land in a feet-together position before attempting to step out.

Basic Description
(1–5) Execute forward handspring with enough power to land you in an erect standing position with a little momentum left over. This can be learned by practicing the handspring to a dive roll onto a crash mat or other soft landing area.

(6–10) Land with slightly bent knees in a fairly balanced position. The more powerful your handspring, the more you can afford to be slightly backward off-balance. Push off the mat with a fast knee extension, and hunch your shoulders forward as if to lead with your lower back during the rotation. Your arm throw (forward and upward) should be coordinated with your head and shoulder movement during the hunching action (see forward somersault). Pike as deeply as you can, and keep your thigh muscles tight to avoid relaxing.

(11–13) A moment after your back has passed the point of being parallel with the floor, split your legs quickly for the step-out. Reach hard to get your lead foot under you so that you do not land in a bent-forward position.

Prerequisites
Strong forward handspring. Tucked forward somersault. Forward handspring to tucked forward somersault to a step-out.

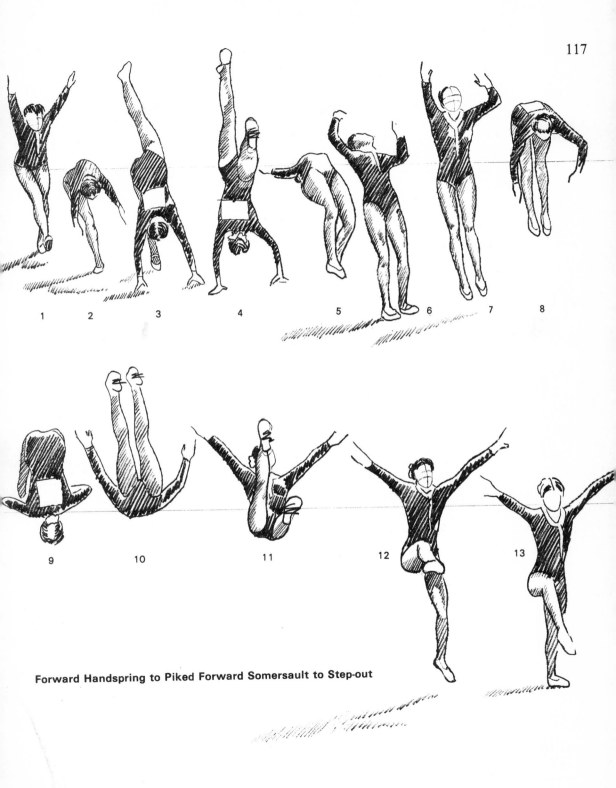

1   2   3   4   5   6   7   8

9   10   11   12   13

Forward Handspring to Piked Forward Somersault to Step-out

Spotting

A very fast spotting hand followed by an equally fast supporting arm is the key to spotting the forward handspring to forward somersault combination.

Forward Handspring to Piked Forward Somersault Spotting

TUCKED BACKWARD SOMERSAULT

Skill Level 7

See instructions for the round-off to backward handspring for an explanation of the two skills that usually precede the backward somersault. However, before attempting a backward somersault from a backward handspring or at the end of a long series, learn to do it from a standing position. You also need lots of experience with the handstand snap-down skill. Good tumblers practice this skill at every training session.

When you perform the preliminary backward handspring, throw your hands backward quickly for a strong snap-down movement of the legs. The snap-down must accelerate the body's movement in preparation for the somersault. In addition, the performer's body position prior to the backward jump is very important. If the upper body position is too low following the backward handspring, there will be a pause between the landing and the jump into the somersault.

Basic Description

(1–8) Throw arms upward and back, and tilt your head and shoulders back slightly. Bring knees toward your chest and over your head, and round your lower back to get your hips tucked under. You may or may not grasp your knees in the tucked position.

(9) Extend hips and legs before landing and keep eyes on the mat.

Tucked Backward Somersault

Prerequisites

Round-off to backward handspring. Standing backward somersault with a spot. Good snap-down from a handstand.

Spotting

This spotting technique insures strong, safe rotation. The spotter must quickly reposition his hands prior to the landing. Spot the performer on many standing backward somersaults before she uses it to end a series. The safest method is to use a spotting belt. If a hand spot must be used, be aware that you must land the performer on her feet and that she may not have prior awareness of the landing. Hand-spot by placing one forearm and hand on the performer's lower back as she jumps, and the other hand under one thigh after the jump. Assist the jump by lifting and guiding the somersault backward. After the performer has turned over (after legs and trunk have passed her head), release your hands and quickly grasp her stomach and back for the landing.

Tucked Backward Somersault Spotting

Piked Backward Somersault (Variation)

Skill Level 8

In performing the piked backward somersault the head is held in a forward position a moment longer than usual. As illustrated, the legs are brought upward toward the head, causing faster backward rotation. The upper body is then rotated backward for the landing.

Piked Backward Somersault

Round-off to Backward Handspring to Layout Backward Somersault to Step-out (Variation)

Skill Level 7

This long series of skills is one of the most commonly employed tumbling series in the floor exercise event. The sequence ends with a layout variation of the backward somersault.

Basic Description

(1–26) Refer to the instructions for the round-off to backward handspring for information about the first two skills in this series. The round-off should be performed rather low to achieve just the right amount of lean for the handspring.

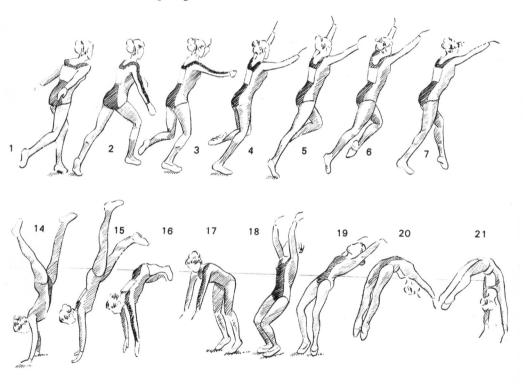

Round-off to Backward Handspring to Layout Backward Somersault to Step-out

(27–30) Throw arms upward and backward after the handspring, holding the head forward until the arms reach shoulder level; the head follows the arms backward after this point. The arms move out to the sides or toward thighs after the backward jump. Tense your seat muscles as you leave the mat and bring your hips upward (without piking). It is important to have a *tight body* during the somersault.

(31–34) Split legs and bring lead foot down on the mat for the landing.

A somewhat more difficult version of the layout backward somersault requires holding the legs together throughout. After you learn the step-out landing, practice keeping the legs together during the layout using the same basic technique.

Prerequisites

Backward handspring and tucked backward somersault. You need the arm thrust of the backward handspring and the elevation of the tucked somersault to perform the layout backward somersault.

Spotting

Use the spotting belt if possible. Hand-spot by supporting the lower back during the first phase, then quickly reposition your hands for the landing phase.

ALTERNATE

Skill Level 9

This series is called an alternate not only because it is the easiest name to give it, but also because it alternates backward handsprings with backward somersaults.

Basic Description

(1–10) Execute a round-off to a backward handspring with a power buildup on the handspring. This series should be performed low and aggressively.

(11–17) Thrust arms early and hard for a layout backward somersault. Although the layout illustrated here is executed high off the mat, it may also be a low, whippy type, which increases the power of the backward drive. The lower "whip back" is similar to a high backward handspring without hands, and insures adequate backward lean for sustained power. Recover from the layout somersault in a piked position so that you can throw backward harder for the ensuing backward handspring. The illustration does not show this position, depicting instead a slightly different (prettier, but not as powerful) style. Which style to use is a decision you will have to make.

(18–22) As with all power backward handsprings, the arms must be thrown back fast and the body kept low to provide body lean and good floor contact. The snap-down from the handstand position should be strong.

(23–30) The momentum is directed upward for the second somersault—this time in the tucked position—by placing the feet slightly behind the hips. All of the other foot placements on landing were slightly in front of the hips to emphasize backward lean.

Alternate

Prerequisites

Round-off to backward handspring and round-off to backward somersault in tucked and layout positions. Ability to execute four backward handsprings with a power buildup.

Spotting

Belt spotting is the safest. Otherwise, use a one-hand spot on the lower back as each part of the series is performed. The spotter must be very prepared for balking; the linkage of this series makes the performer susceptible to a change of mind at the last moment. Teach the performer to watch the mat after each somersault to be sure she does not attempt to begin the handspring before landing after the somersault.

PIKED ARABIAN SOMERSAULT TO STEP-OUT

Skill Level 8

This skill is a forward somersault that begins with a half twist. It should be learned in a tucked position before proceeding to a piked position. You should also learn it with your feet together on the landing before attempting the step-out.

Basic Description

(1–2) This skill may be initiated from a round-off or backward handspring.
(3–5) Thrust arms and hips upward as in the layout backward somersault. As

Piked Arabian Somersault to Step-out

you spring off your feet, pull one shoulder backward (leading with your elbow) in the direction of the twist, turn head under armpit, and throw other arm in direction of twist. Try to see the mat for an instant after the twist and before the somersault.

(6–8) Pike sharply after the twist by thrusting arms and upper body downward and under toward legs. Try to develop a feeling of leading with the lower back while turning over.

(9–11) Extend hips before landing. Step out by splitting legs and reaching under your body for the floor with lead leg. Be sure you step out with the leg that will enable you to go right into a handspring or round-off if you wish to continue tumbling.

Prerequisites

Layout backward somersault. Arabian (half twist) dive roll. Tucked and piked front somersault on mat or trampoline.

Spotting

Use the spotting belt if possible. Hand-spot by standing on the side that corresponds to the direction of the twist. If it is a left half twist, allow performer to roll the twist onto your left arm. Then reach across her back with other arm and assist rotation. This method may be modified according to the experience of the spotter and the gymnast. It would be prudent to land the performer on a soft, thick crash mat. The spotter should bear in mind that the step-out leg should be the leg the performer uses to launch into handsprings and round-offs.

8   9   10   11

Layout Arabian Somersault to Step-out (Variation)

Skill Level 9

Split your legs as much as possible to facilitate forward rotation. Do not avoid any of the prerequisites for this skill.

Basic Description

(1–3) Execute a low, powerful round-off or round-off to a backward hand-spring. Either start should end with a strong pushing action off the mat, assisted by an upward thrust of the arms. Your arms should be high when you take off so that you can get them into the thrusting pattern early. Holding arms low or bringing them up late will cause you to twist around laterally rather than "over the top," and any sideways motion will upset your balance during the landing. As you raise your arms, look under the armpit of the arm that corresponds to

Layout Arabian Somersault to Step-out   **6**

the direction of twist. Avoid twisting early and slighting the push with the legs into the jump.

(4–9) A slight piking action usually occurs as the twist and somersault are initiated. The lead leg is lifted sharply overhead for the aerial somersault, but the head and chest must be stabilized. If you continue to bend at the waist to increase your rotation, you will end up doing a piked somersault instead of a layout somersault. This phase of the skill —leading with the leg instead of the chest—gives a very different feeling than you get from most somersault movements. Spread your arms to the sides after the twist to aid forward rotation and to stop the twisting action. As you turn over, watch the mat as you would during an aerial forward somersault.

(10–11) Reach for the mat as hard as you can with the landing leg throughout rotation, and keep your thigh muscles tight. Step out as in an aerial walkover.

Prerequisites

Piked arabian dive roll. Aerial forward walkover. Layout forward somersault on trampoline or off springboard onto crash mat.

Spotting

Stand on the side that corresponds to the twisting direction. Here, assume that performer is executing a right twist, and spotter is standing on the right side. Reach under performer's stomach with right arm (palm up) as takeoff occurs. To avoid inhibiting performer, do not touch her until the half twist is almost completed. The performer should roll the twist onto spotter's forearm. Assist rotation by lifting with your right arm and supporting lower back area with left arm. You may hold on with both hands and finish with a crossed-arm grasp or release your right arm from the performer's stomach and grasp her left arm. Either way, be sure to land the performer softly.

BACKWARD SOMERSAULT WITH FULL RIGHT TWIST

Skill Level 10

It is a good idea to first learn this somersault on the trampoline in a twisting spotting belt. Have the technique firmly in mind before proceeding to the mat. If you are unable to do a good layout backward somersault, you will probably have some difficulty learning this skill. Execute this skill from a round-off or backward handspring.

Backward Somersault with Full Right Twist (Side View)

When a full twist is done, the upper body usually tends toward a backward lean and twist as the feet leave the floor. A poor full-twisting somersault is often marked by too much twisting at the moment of takeoff; the head is tilted back severely and a half twist has occurred before the feet have left the mat. Learn to spring vigorously into the somersault before twisting. Somersault thrust should always take precedence over twisting motion, since there is a natural tendency among beginners to overemphasize twisting drive to the detriment of the somersault.

Basic Description

(1–3) Throw arms up and back as in the layout backward somersault, and incline your left arm toward the right. Try to avoid throwing your head back until the arms are well above shoulder level. Hips should be tucked under, with seat muscles tensed to keep the body rigid. Pull your right elbow and shoulder to the right as your body approaches a horizontal position. At the same time, turn your head to the right (try to focus your eyes on the mat at this point) and throw your left arm across your chest to the right.

(4–7) Continue twisting until you sense (or see) that you are approaching the mat. Extend arms to the sides to stop twisting rotation, and land with feet together. A diagonal view of this somersault clearly shows that the mat may be observed throughout the somersault after the twist has been initiated.

Backward Somersault with Full Twist (Diagonal View)

Prerequisites

Layout backward somersault. A backward somersault with a half twist is desirable but not necessary.

Spotting

The spotter must quickly support the performer's lower back, aid the twist during flight, and land the performer gently. Use of a spotting belt with overhead rigging is strongly recommended. Hand-spot from the side that corresponds to the direction of the twist. (Some spotters prefer the other side.)

After supporting the gymnast's back as she leaps backward, place your right arm (in the case of a right twist) across her stomach as she rolls into your arm during the first half twist. Support and/or push the performer "over the top." As she passes through an inverted position, reach around her right hip with your left forearm, aid the twist, and support the landing phase.

Backward Somersault with Full Right Twist Spotting

4

Dance and the Floor Exercise Event

Various dance skills are used in two of the four Olympic gymnastic events for women: the floor exercise and balance beam events. There are no restrictions on the kinds of dance movements performed or on dance style in gymnastics. You may combine a classic ballet movement with the most abstract and asymmetrical dance maneuvers that you can conceive. The most important consideration is to integrate and harmonize your dance movements with your gymnastic skills to create a pleasing, aesthetic overall performance.

Most gymnastics coaches agree that combining formal dance training with gymnastic practice is important. Dance training will help you understand various postures and poses, enabling you to project a desired emotion while performing. It is strongly recommended that the beginning gymnast enroll in a dance class to supplement her gymnastic training.

Since the subject of dance is too vast to explain thoroughly here, the following is a discussion of *selected* dance positions and movements.

133

Learn to stand erect with your hips partially tucked under, with abdomen taut and buttocks firm. Hold your pelvic area in a medial position so that it does not bulge outward in the rear or protrude in front. Relax your shoulders without slouching forward, and hold your head in an erect position. These rules must be kept in mind for good posture during a performance.

As you stand and move, you must be able to rotate your legs (180 degrees is ideal) without disturbing hip alignment. There should be no awkward angles formed by the arms and hands. Elbows and wrists have very subtle curves; never allow these soft curves to disappear. The fingers should assume a soft, rounded position. The thumb is held under, and the index finger is slightly separated from the other fingers. The third finger is positioned somewhat lower than the others and all fingers are held slightly apart.

Some Basic Positions

All steps and movements relate to one or more of the following basic positions. Practice in front of a mirror and examine each position from the front and side.

First Position
The heels and knees touch, and the feet form a straight line. Arms are curved and held low, with the fingertips barely touching the thighs.

Second Position

The heels are about twelve inches apart. The arms are extended in a curved line slightly below and in front of the shoulders.

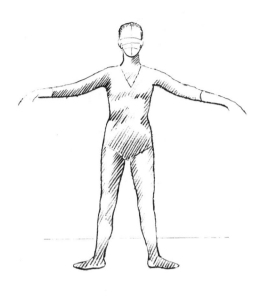

Third Position

The legs are turned outward, with one foot in front of the other. The heel of each foot is adjacent to the middle of the other foot. Either arm may be raised; the other arm is held as in the preceding position. Keep your shoulder down as you raise your arm.

Fourth Position

The legs are turned outward, with one foot a short step in front of the other. Either arm may be held in the near-horizontal position. The other arm crosses the body in front of the ribs, palm facing the body.

Fifth Position: Arms Low

One foot is placed directly in front of the other. The heel of the front foot is held against the joint of the big toe of the rear foot.

Fifth Position: Arms High

The arms may be held low, in front, or high. They form a circle, with the hands several inches apart.

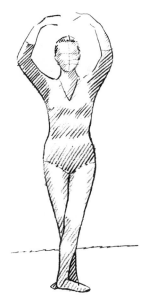

These descriptions are abbreviated and provide only a rudimentary understanding of basic ballet stances. The reader should make a further investigation of these basic positions.

Demi-plié

The demi-plié (de-mee-plee-AY) is a half-bend of the knees used in ballet as a preparatory position for jumping movements and most steps. Pliés should be practiced daily using all positions of the feet. This exercise will help give you the leg flexibility and strength needed to perform light, springy jumps.

Spread your feet and distribute your weight evenly between them. Grasp a bar to maintain balance if necessary. Your heels never leave the floor during this exercise. Bend your knees in a direct line with the toes until the stretch in the calf muscle prevents further lowering without lifting your heels. Return to the starting position. Your spine must be held straight (hips partially tucked under) throughout this exercise. This is a smooth, slow movement without pauses.

Demi-plié

Relevé

The relevé (reh-luh-VAY) will help strengthen your legs and promote a secure demi-pointe (ball of the foot) position for balance skills, turns, and other dance movements. Perform the relevé by rising slowly on your toes in all positions of the feet. Rise to the halfway point without bending your knees. Return to the starting position. Combine the plié with the relevé in all positions of the feet. This exercise should be practiced while holding onto a hip-level bar and looking into a mirror. The relevés can also be practiced on one foot. The balanced position on the toes, with weight properly distributed, is of great value in floor exercise and balance beam dance.

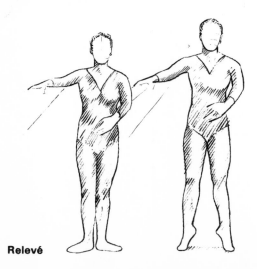

Relevé

Walking

Walking movements should be performed as if you are gliding across the floor. As each step is executed, the leg should be turned slightly outward from the hip, with toes pointed. Hold your body erect (stomach tight and hips half-tucked) so that your seat does not protrude in the rear. Hold your head erect and keep your shoulders down and relaxed. Your elbows should not be rigid and your wrists should not be limp. The ball of the foot is placed on the floor, rather than the heel as in normal walking. The arms may swing in opposition to each step or be held out to the side.

Your walking pattern may be varied by changing levels (dipping), moving sideways (crossing legs), walking backward, or adding other body movements if desired.

The tempo of your walk may also be varied to create a certain impression or simply to provide variation. If you walk fast, you are in a hurry. Slow, even walking suggests caution, and a change of rhythm may be jazzy or modern in appearance.

Illustrated here is an intricate walking pattern that combines body wave, a slight change in elevation, and asymmetrical arm movement, suggesting perhaps an awakening, a blossoming, or a revelation.

Walking

The following illustration demonstrates a walking step that utilizes extreme hip, shoulder, and knee movement to convey a jazz theme.

Another Walking Pattern

Running

Running is usually used in the floor exercise to create power for a tumbling skill such as a round-off or forward handspring. Running is also used to show a strong linear movement across the floor, performed with erect upper body posture and head held in a natural position, or with variations in body position and pace, as in walking. You may, however, run in a circular pattern, backward, or with a modified body position designed to suggest a particular mood

Running

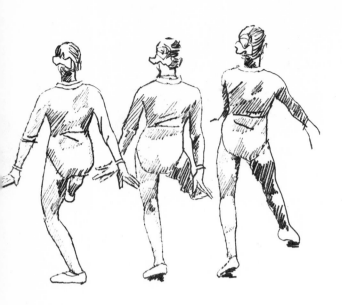

or function. The pace of the music you choose for your floor exercise will help you decide the speed, pattern, and body position of the run. Your running strides should be even, with your arms swinging normally in opposition to each stride.

This illustration shows a gymnast turning into a running pattern that demonstrates change of pace, slight body wave and twist, and expressive extension and retraction of the arms.

Jumps, Hops, and Leaps

Jumps, hops, and leaps are light, elevated movements that start from a one- or two-foot takeoff and finish on one or both feet. The thrust of the legs must be fast, powerful, and complete to gain maximum elevation. After the initial thrust from the mat, the body should immediately move into the desired position, and at the apex of flight the viewer should have a clear impression of the distinctive character of the jump, hop, or leap. The landing is performed by lowering from the ball of the foot to the heel with a simultaneous bending of the hip and knee joints to absorb the shock. Inhale before leaving the mat, hold your breath in flight, and exhale after landing.

Jumps

Jumps are vertical and/or linear movements that may be executed from both feet to both feet, from both feet to one foot, or from one foot to both feet. Practice some of the following jumps by starting in a standing position, bending your knees, and performing each jump both forward and backward.

Bent-Knee Jump from One Foot to Both Feet

Notice the slight shrug of the shoulders and change of head position during the jump, with eyes looking to the right, then forward, and finally to the left.

Bent-Knee Jump

Short Straddle Jump Forward

Spring from both feet and land on both feet.

Straddle Jump

Jump with Full Twist from One Foot to Two
The arms and lead leg are extended upward at the same time to attain enough altitude to complete the twist.

Jump with Full Twist

Hops

A hop is a springing movement from one foot to a landing on the same foot. It is usually preceded by a walking or step-out skill. Execute a series of small hops on one foot and then the other. Practice skipping across the floor forward and backward, lifting the knee of your raised leg high and keeping your toes pointed. Try to hop as high as you can each time.

Step Hop with Leg Held Rearward

Hop as high as possible. As you improve, split your legs wider, experimenting with arm, head, and leg positions but retaining the same basic hop. Your ingenuity may create unique movements, which are necessary in a well-choreographed floor exercise routine.

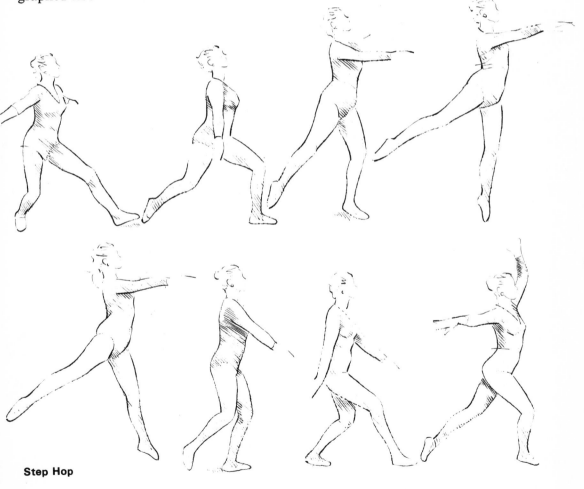

Step Hop

Hop and Switch Legs to Split Position

Do not expect to immediately master this skill. You must have excellent flexibility in both a right and left leg split position and the strength to briefly hold your legs in the split position in mid-air.

Hop, Switch Legs, and Split

Lateral Hop to Wide Straddle Position

This hop can be turned into a side leap by pushing off the mat with one foot and landing on the other.

Lateral Hop to Straddle

Hop with Bent Rear Knee

The closer the rear foot is brought to the head, the more exciting the hop.

Bent-Knee Hop

Back Cabriole

In this hop, one leg is held rearward and the hopping leg is thrust back against it, pushing it even higher rearward.

Back Cabriole

Front Cabriole

Here one leg is thrust forward (as in a basic hop with straight leg) and the hopping leg follows and strikes its underside, sending it higher into the air.

Front Cabriole

Leaps

A leap is a springing movement from one foot to a landing on the other foot. Perform a basic leap from a slow run. Step forward with a slightly bent knee and thrust your rear leg forward and upward. Straighten both legs and point your toes in flight. Land on your forward foot (the ball of the foot and then the heel) with a slight bending of your knee and hip to absorb the shock.

Now try some of the following leaps.

Pas de Chat

The pas de chat (pa-duh-SHA), or cat leap, was so named because of its similarity to the springing movements of a cat. Adding a half twist or full twist creates an interesting variation.

Pas de Chat

Chassé

A chassé (sha-SAY) is basically a gallop step. One foot is placed forward and is displaced by the other foot. This leap is frequently used in combination with jumps, hops, and tumbling skills.

Chassé

Tour Jeté

In the tour jeté (tur-zuh-TAY), one leg is kicked upward, a half turn is executed, and the legs are switched so that the landing occurs on the foot of the kicking leg. It is important to complete the initial leg thrust before turning.

Tour Jeté

Split Leap

In the split leap style illustrated here, the gymnast lifts the front knee until it is level with the hip. After takeoff the legs are extended to a split position. Keeping the rear leg up in this split position is difficult; however, your strength can be improved by exercise.

Split Leap

Split Leap with Bent Knees

The split leap with bent knees depicted here is begun toward the end of a full turn. Both legs are bent in this type of split leap. The gymnast has chosen to continue the turn after landing.

Bent-Knees Split Leap

Leap with Full Twist

The leap with full twist shown in this illustration is performed with alternate bending of the knees, and is followed by a half turn that ends in a deep lunge position.

Leap with Full Twist

Turns and Pirouettes

Turns and pirouettes are extremely difficult dance elements because of the high degree of balance required for correct execution. Turns require somewhat less balance because they are done on both feet or alternating feet. Pirouettes are performed on one foot. Both turns and pirouettes may be performed from either a kneeling or a squatting position.

Spotting

"Spotting" a fixed point during turning and pirouetting is an important consideration in the correct execution of these movements. Spotting in dance should not be confused with spotting (physically assisting the performer) in gymnastics. Dance spotting is a technique that aids balance while spinning. As the spin is begun, the eyes are focused on a fixed point located in the near distance at eye level. As the body continues to spin, the head momentarily remains stationary as the eyes continue to watch the "spot" as long as possible. Then the head is whipped around 360 degrees in the direction of the turn and the eyes respot the original fixed point before the body has completed a full circle. This procedure is repeated with each ensuing turn or pirouette.

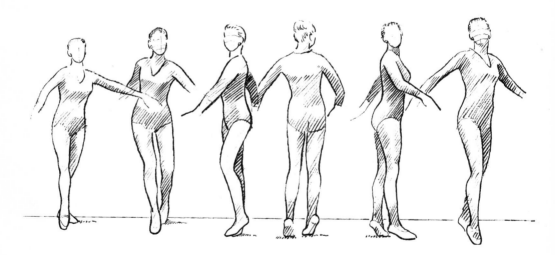

Spotting in a Turn

Turns may be begun with the feet in either the first position or fifth position (described earlier). You may turn in place or travel in any direction. All turns should be executed with a rising action on the balls of the feet.

Pirouettes (one-foot turns) require lots of practice because your balance and posture must be almost perfect. Following are some examples of inward and outward pirouettes, performed in various styles.

Spotting While Performing an Inward Pirouette
Turn in the direction that corresponds to your support leg. This illustration shows a turn to the left with the left leg supporting the body.

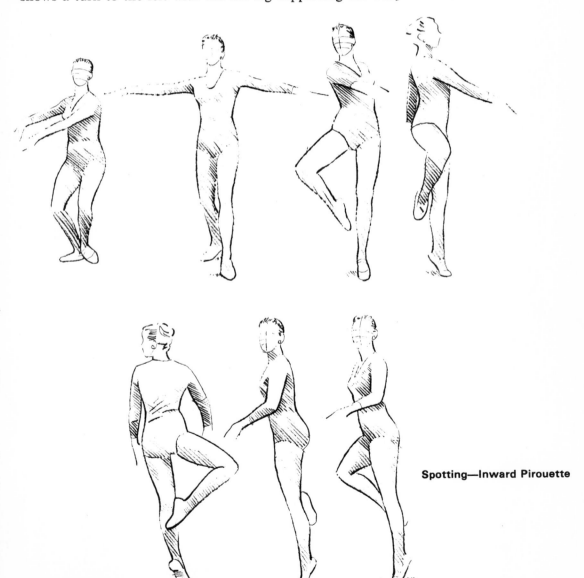

Spotting—Inward Pirouette

Spotting While Performing an Outward Pirouette

Turn in the direction that corresponds to your raised leg. This illustration shows a turn to the right with the left leg supporting the body.

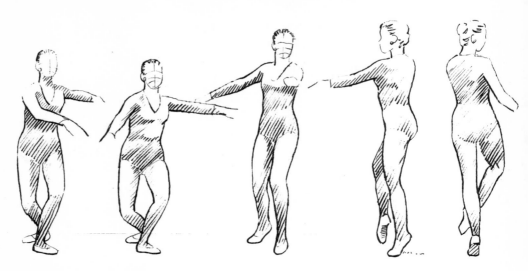

Spotting—Outward Pirouette

Inward Pirouette

The character or jazz style of this inward pirouette suits the mood of this particular routine.

Inward Pirouette

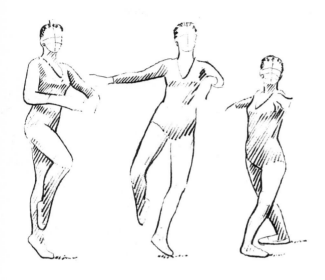

Skater's Inward Pirouette

This kind of pirouette is usually associated with figure skating.

Skater's Inward Pirouette

Double Inward Pirouette with Bent Knee

Double Inward Pirouette

Outward Pirouette with Jazz Flavor

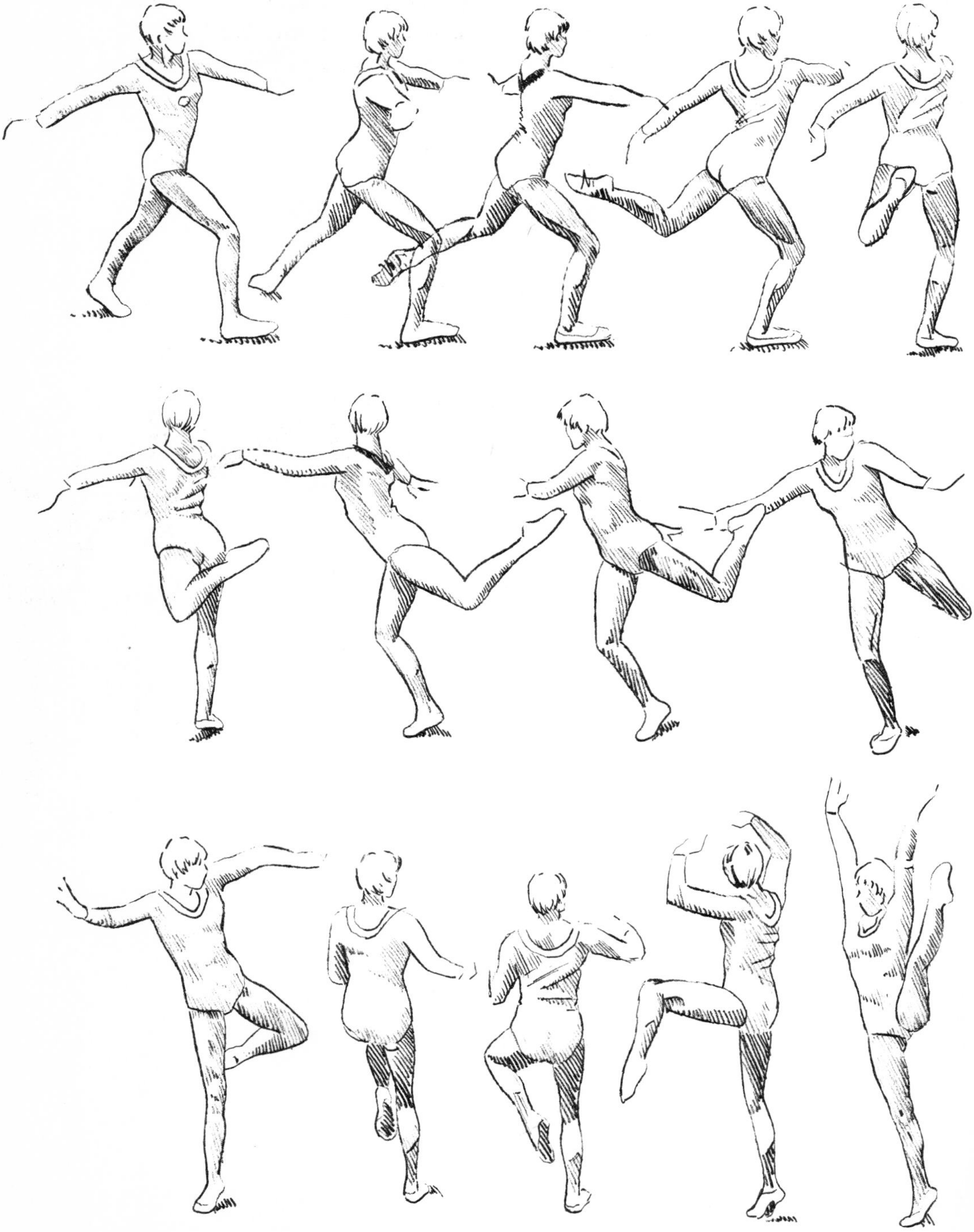

Outward Pirouette

The gymnast is free to modify certain dance positions and movements to suit her body type or personal style. This privilege is often used as a substitute for correct technique or otherwise abused, but after the performer has learned all the dance skills in the classical manner, she may choose alternatives. For example, following are three variations of the tour jeté.

This is a more or less classical ballet tour jeté.

Here the kicking leg is bent and the other leg finishes in a forward position.

In this tour jeté, both legs are bent prior to landing. The rear leg remains bent as the gymnast lands.

5

Selected Floor Exercise Combinations

New combinations of skills are constantly invented by gymnasts and coaches. The beginning gymnast, of course, should learn the basics before attempting to be innovative. The purpose of this chapter is to present some common combinations to be practiced, and to show the beginning gymnast how skills are combined in a routine. Included are a few new skills as well as some slightly modified versions of familiar tumbling movements. The numerical system of rating skills according to their difficulty will allow the student to choose skill combinations she can handle and that will be fun to practice.

These selected floor exercise combinations include movements that bring into contact with the mat not only the hands and feet, as in tumbling, but other parts of the body as well. Such movements usually appear at least once in every good floor exercise routine, enabling the performer to radically change elevation, demonstrate flexibility, introduce balance elements, change direction, and perform slower-moving skills. These maneuvers and their numerous variations add interest and excitement to otherwise predictable tumbling runs.

Remember, like all of the others the following illustrations are of some of the best gymnasts in the world. Do not be surprised if they make it look easy.

Fall to Leg Turns to Split and Turns to Kneedle

A stretched pose into a low, backward fall followed by leg circling and rolling through a split position that eventually ends in another split position. This sequence demonstrates a change of elevation, imaginative combination, and extreme flexibility.

Fall to Leg Turns to Split and Turns to Kneedle

Falling Half Turn to Front Support, Kick to Half Turn to Sit

An elevated hop to a backward fall and turn combination that climaxes in an unusual handstand falling sequence. This exercise demonstrates changes of elevation, unusual combination, and imagination.

Falling Half Turn to Front Support, Kick to Half Turn to Sit

Handstand Arch-over to Feet

A kick to a handstand and arch-over to a stand is an example of a basic sequence used to show extreme flexibility and control.

Sit to Valdez to Chest Roll

From a sitting position to a backward arch to a handstand to a chest roll. This combination shows flexibility and balance.

Backward Roll Shoot to Handstand to Split

A backward roll and shoot to a split handstand, then down to a split is another display of balance and flexibility.

Backward Roll Shoot to Handstand to Split

Split to Forward Turn and Roll to Back

This transition from a split to a roll includes a pose and arm support.

Split to Forward Turn and Roll to Back

Split, Swing Arms to Knee Scale

Sliding up to one knee from a split position is a simple way to get back on your feet.

Split, Swing Arms to Knee Scale

Falling Half Turn to Backward Shoulder Roll to Knee

A fall and half turn to a backward roll to a knee scale is a perfect example of a basic skill performed from an imaginative starting position.

Falling Half Turn to Backward Shoulder Roll to Knee

Knee Spin

A knee spin can be an exciting movement if your arms are used to enhance the motion.

Knee Spin

Back Spin

Here is an example of a double back spin with exciting changes of leg positions. The back spin can be used to change direction.

Back Spin

Arm Swing with Dip and Hop to Corner

A sideways body wave coupled with a hop allows the performer to move a little deeper into the far corner of the floor exercise area, providing more space for her dismount.

**Arm Swing with Dip
and Hop to Corner**

Forward Walkover Turn to Knee Scale

A turn out of a forward walkover to a knee scale is a flexibility skill that often provides an element of surprise.

Forward Walkover Turn to Knee Scale

Chest Roll to Chest Stand

This forward chest roll to a chest stand exhibits flexibility and balance.

Chest Roll to Chest Stand

Split to Backward Turn

A backward turn from a split allows the gymnast to change direction and move into another floor pattern.

Split to Backward Turn

Full Turn on Heels to Fall, Full Turn to Support

An unusual starting position is followed by a full turn into a fall, with an additional full turn incorporating sitting and support positions. The hooked toes and body angles suggest a jazz sequence.

Full Turn on Heels to Fall, Full Turn to Support